The MNM Team Building Process For Printers

Michael P. O'Connor

Becky Erickson

OLD STONE PUBLISHING

PORTLAND, MAINE

All of the company names used in the examples in
this book are fictitious. Any resemblance to
real companies is purely coincidental.

Published by
OLD STONE PUBLISHING
P.O. Box 7572 · Portland, Maine 04112 · (207) 772-8886

Cover design by John Kramer / Imageset Design / Portland, Maine

Library of Congress Catalog Card Number: 91-090250
ISBN 0-9629366-7-7

Printed in the United States of America

To my family and the countless friends, clients, and colleagues who have
given me the opportunity to learn about life.

M.P.O.

■

To my parents

for giving me the opportunity to learn about printing.

B.E.

CONTENTS

FIGURES

THE

MNM

Team Building

Process

for

Printers

INTRODUCTION

During the coming decade, the information and technology explosion which began in the 1980s will intensify. The impact of this explosion upon small business in general—and upon the printing industry in particular—will be dramatic. As a result, traditional economic indicators and forecasting tools will become less reliable due to the increasing complexity and uncertainty of many new variables.

In the past, printshop owners could, for the most part, pick and choose the products, services, customers and overall direction that their business would take. Growth was predictable, customers' needs and schedules were easily accommodated, and technological improvements could be planned and budgeted. The work force was stable and dependable. Remember? It wasn't really too long ago.

Today, successfully meeting the demands of your customers requires a greater flexibility and elasticity in company policy and personnel than ever before. Old responses of "that's not the way we do it" are being replaced by various versions of "how can we help you?" and "we're glad to do it your way."

In the future, every printing business, regardless of size or location, will be more and more market driven. Increasingly, it will be your *customer*, not you, the owner, who determines what products your business offers. And, your customer will dictate how and when these products and services will be provided! The reason, of course, is the shift to the Information Age. Bye, bye smokestacks. Hello megabytes, fax, and color copiers.

To better understand the changes that are taking place and will continue to take place, it is worthwhile to consider the *changing role and function* of the printshop in the business community. In a very real sense, the role and function of the everyday printshop has changed dramatically during the shift from the Industrial Age to the Information Age. During the Industrial Age, the role of the printshop was *useful, supportive* and *peripheral*. In the Information

Age this role has become *critical, integral* and *central.* The printshop that once was a hard-to-find dark and dirty producer of letterheads, envelopes, and tickets has today become one of the most useful, utilized and important suppliers to businesses of all sizes. Many customers who once hadn't a clue about how printing was produced, today are almost as educated as the printshop owners.

If predictability and stability were fundamental to the Industrial Age printshop, what will be the nature of the Information Age printshop?

For one thing, this new printshop will be *fast* … very fast. The ability to produce quickly will become critical. Alvin Toffler, in his book *Powershifts,* speaks convincingly of the need for businesses to be able to speed up every aspect of production and service. As Toffler puts it, businesses will have "to operate at the pace of those in a position to buy." In short, they will have to "rev up or drop out." Certainly this will be true for printshops. And this revving up will involve much more than increasing productivity and shortening delivery times. It will also mean *attaining a sustainable and dependable high level of quality.* In the Information Age *every* eye becomes a trained eye and total quality becomes an accepted norm in both product and service.

How is this increased productivity and excellence in quality to be achieved? Innovation in technology will set the pace. Ever-changing and increasingly user-friendly technology will continue to stretch the capacities and capabilities of the small and mid-size printshops. Both the owner's talents for creative financing and the staff's ability to learn effective utilization of new technology will be pushed to the max. Yes, without question, to remain competitive will assume state-of-the-art technological competency.

Having the right equipment, however, cannot guarantee increased productivity and quality. Far from it. There is another critical ingredient, and that is people. Here is where the Information Age printshop meets its biggest challenge.

Technology will not determine the quality of a printshop's competitive edge because the new technology will be available to all and all will have it (at least all who are serious players). The difference will be, as it has always been, *people.* Like the new technology, the personnel of the Information Age printshop will have little in common with the personnel of the Industrial Age printshop. Styles of management, decision making, inter-staff relationships, customer and vendor relationships, will all change. Concepts such as company mission and vision, self-managing teams, efficiency, innovation, flexibility, communication, consistency, responsibility and pride in work will become the pathways and the measuring sticks for a printshop's success.

This book is about the people part of the Information Age printshop equation ... the owners, employees, customers, vendors. It is about new ways of working, communicating, and growing together to develop a high-performance team capable of increasing your productivity and improving your quality. This book is also about other less measurable, but certainly no less tangible or desirable, issues such as building your printshop into an exciting, more enjoyable and less stressful business where you and your employees can come to engage in meaningful work. It's about creating a business which is seen by its customers and vendors as an important and valuable resource and asset to the community. And it's about new ways of doing business which, ultimately, will increase not only your overall sales, but your bottom line as well.

In the final analysis, this book is a *how-to* book, or to be more accurate, a *how to be your own printshop effectiveness consultant*. In writing the book it has been our goal to present the material in a way that allows us to take this journey of improvement with you, exploring each of the ideas and challenges together. The material should not be viewed as a template or fixed process in which every step must be closely adhered to if success is to be achieved. Instead, we hope this material will serve as a road map for an in-depth and serious, yet playful, exploration of a process where you and your employees can determine just what it is that your company, its people, products and services really stand for. We firmly believe that one size does *not* fit all and encourage you to modify The MNM Team Building Process to suit *your* needs, *your* personality, and *your* creativity.

The MNM Process alone will not lead to a truly successful printing business. Your people can be the most efficient team in the world, but you'll never realize their potential if you aren't continually learning and practicing sound business management skills and expanding your knowledge of the printing industry. We encourage you to explore and learn whatever skills you need to make managing your business an exciting daily event.

We see the completion of The MNM Process as another step in your on-going improvement cycle. We hope that what you learn from this book will lead to ever-expanding levels of learning, understanding, and satisfaction in your professional work and daily life in the years to come.

What To Expect From This Book

Simply stated, the goal of this book is to present a tested and proven method which you can implement yourself, that will significantly increase productivity and improve quality within your printing business through greater utilization of your greatest asset … people. We've called this method The MNM Team Building Process.

What *Is* The MNM Team Building Process, Anyway, and What Is It Based On?

The MNM Team Building Process presents and utilizes a synthesis of the best of current ideas, concepts and strategies which have proven effective in developing more productive and innovative teams of motivated people. The process is very flexible and is designed so you can tailor the program to fit your specific needs and staff.

The major concepts which are a part of The MNM Team Building Process include:

- Self-managing Work Teams
- Personal Management and Decision Making Styles
- Total Quality Systems for Product and Service
- Alignment of Short-term Action Plans and Long-term Strategies

The approach taken in The MNM Team Building Process is an applied approach, rather than a theoretical approach. (That means that we expect you to *do* things as we go along!) Our book is written for busy owners like yourself who have little time to waste in trying to separate useful approaches from an excess of philosophical and theoretical jargon. The process is developed around basic concepts which can be implemented in a step-by-step manner, at *your* pace, as *your* schedule allows, over a time frame of several months.

As you go through The MNM Process, there may be times when you might desire a better understanding of the theory and background behind the concepts you are using. This information can be found in The MNM Tool Kit. The Tool Kit also provides reference material on related concepts, ideas and resources which you might find useful later as you expand and continue The MNM Process.

The heart of The MNM Process is the meetings you will have with your staff, and it's from these meetings that the process takes its name. "MNM" is an acronym for "Monday Night Meetings." It seems that for most of the groups we've worked with, Monday night was always the best night for the staff to meet (fewer conflicts and more energy). So people—ourselves included—always referred to the group work as the "Monday Night Meetings" or "MNMs."

How Effective Will The MNM Team Building Process Be For My Business?

It is rare that any business strategy proves to be universally effective. Businesses, like the individuals who own them and the people who staff them, develop unique personalities. To illustrate this point, think for a moment about several printshops that you are familiar with—perhaps competitors or maybe those of friends or acquaintances. Now, thinking of each of the businesses as a living, breathing entity, list all the one-word adjectives you feel accurately describe the *personality* of each business (not the personality of the owner or staff, or the facilities and equipment, but the business itself). Think of this as being similar to describing to a stranger several people whom you know quite well. Done? Good. Now do it for your own business. Now compare them. Are they the same? You probably found some differences. Maybe they were *all* different. Just as the personality of each business differs, so will The MNM Process yield considerably different results for every business that goes through it.

The MNM Process is not a template or a series of hoops which are designed to produce a specific result or change in a company. Instead, the process is designed to meet your business and its people *where they are*, and then use team oriented and team building approaches to explore and develop strategies for improvement that are totally *unique* and *appropriate* for *your* company. Each company's path along the process will be different; yet just as we as individuals retain our identity as we grow and mature, so will your company.

With these thoughts in mind, you can see that the answer to the question,

How effective will The MNM Team Building Process be for my business? is difficult to predict. It's sort of like asking a major league football team at the beginning of pre-season practice how it will finish the year! It's going to depend on many variables.

Not a sufficient answer? Need some real numbers? Okay, as a business person, these are valid questions. Here are some answers based on the experience of other companies who have implemented the concepts and strategies outlined in The MNM Process.

Qualitatively speaking, with very few exceptions, The MNM Process will yield *significant* improvement in production and quality. And, this, of course, translates into increased sales and profits. In terms of hard numbers, we're probably looking at bottom line gross sales *minimum* increases of 10 to 15%. In her own shop, the co-author of this book realized an increase of 20% within *six months* of implementing The MNM Process. Maximum? Again, very difficult, but as reported in the article "Who Needs A Boss?" in the May 1990 issue of "Fortune" magazine, many companies are reporting figures of 40% or better where self-managing work teams have had a chance to really settle in.

You alone, of course, will determine how well your company will improve.

How Long and How Much Effort Will It Take?

Probably the most accurate answer is forever and continuous.

The MNM Team Building Process is, at its fullest implementation, an on-going process of *continuous improvement*, not only for your staff, but for your entire company. But rather than frighten you too much, maybe a better answer (at least at this stage of the discussion) is that you will need one two-hour block of time once every two weeks in which you and all shop staff members are present. Utilizing a bi-weekly meeting schedule such as this, you can expect to work through the Phase III creative and implementation portion of the process (see figure 2.1) in about six or eight months, with an actual time involvement of approximately 30 to 40 hours. Phases IV and V, the on-going improvement and monitoring part of the process, would normally continue indefinitely, but with less frequent staff meetings, maybe once every three weeks.

This brings us to another concept that lies at the core of the process outlined in this book—the concept of short-term versus long-term gain. The MNM Process *will* yield remarkable short-term increases in productivity and improvement in quality. Yet this is *not* part of the primary goal. Rather, the focus is based on achieving continuous and sustainable improvements over a longer period of time. Quick-fix business improvement systems are like many of the so-called "miracle" diet systems: big on promises, but frustratingly ineffective. Even if you possess great personal willpower and desire, this process is not one which you could implement overnight even if you knew all the steps by heart.

No, The MNM process will take time. Why? Because *you are building a team*. And any time you start working for change utilizing groups of people, you must expect the process to take a longer period of time than if you were only trying to change yourself.

In terms of how much effort is involved, the answer is one of those good news/bad news situations. The good news is that other than finding a meeting time acceptable to all of your staff, the time element will not be a problem. Neither you as facilitator nor your fledgling team will need to spend a lot of time or effort in preparation or follow-up of the actual meetings.

Minimal homework! Great! What's the bad news?

The difficulties in implementing The MNM Process are complementary in nature and actually are the two opposite sides of the same coin. For the shop owner, the greatest difficulty will be in dealing with the fear that you are *losing or giving up control*. For your employees, it will be the fear of assuming more accountability and responsibility. Both fears are real and natural, yet when approached gently and gradually (two hours a week, every two weeks) progress will be achieved. Is the work hard? You bet. Is it all worth it? In retrospect, certainly—although during the process there probably will be times when you may wonder.

The bottom-line reason for all of the difficulty, be it yours or on the part of your people, is that in this process we are dealing with changing both the thoughts and perceptions of the way people work and should work together. The degree to which these changes are perceived as problems will vary from shop to shop and person to person.

Again, the experiences and results of implementing The MNM Process will be unique for every business.

How Will We Know When We're Achieving Results?

Although the implementation of The MNM Team Building Process is spread over several months, you can expect to see initial results almost immediately. These results will manifest themselves in many small ways. One of the first signs is an increase in the "smile factor." Not only will you and your employees be smiling more, but *so will your customers*—even during those over-load times of increased stress!

Another early sign will be more willingness and flexibility on the part of your staff to communicate over jobs. For example, complex jobs that typically require a long time to produce or are particularly demanding in terms of quality requirements will begin to move through the system more quickly, and with fewer hassles or mistakes. This may even happen without your presence being required! Now, that's a scary thought!

What would you do if one day you, expecting the worst, asked your staff what was the status of Precise Engineering's order (habitually a very demanding and difficult-to-satisfy, yet financially valuable, customer), and were told that it was finished and delivered! Well, you'd better think about it, because this *will* happen. If you missed seeing that job go out on time, you would definitely not miss this event (which one graduate of The MNM process actually experienced): the delivery of a huge flower arrangement from Precise Engineering in appreciation for excellent performance on a difficult job well done! So, you needn't worry about seeing results. They will begin showing themselves very quickly after the process begins.

But, you say, how can this be? How can such results be achieved so soon? How can people be taught how to do this in such a short time? The answer is that in The MNM Process people don't have to be *taught* much of anything! This fact is actually one of the core concepts: *people, for the most part, already know the right thing to do.* The reason they don't always do the right thing is that they haven't been asked or the business system itself doesn't permit them.

What Are the Specific Results and Benefits of The MNM Process?

Numerous books have been written in the past several years around the central theme of excellence in business—*In Search of Excellence* by Tom Peters and Robert Waterman, Jr., *On Becoming A Leader*, by Warren Bennis, and *The Change Masters*, by Rosabeth Moss Kanter. In studying the companies and the successful techniques that these books describe, one very simple, yet apparently critical strategy which they all seem to have in common is that they consistently focus on business practices which benefit *all of the stakeholders*. By stakeholders we mean any person or group of people connected in some way to the company—owners, management, employees, customers, vendors—even the community at large.

To neglect any of these stakeholders, these companies would argue, would initiate a downward slide towards mediocrity or worse. While all of us know companies that continue to ignore some of their stakeholders yet continue to thrive, the signs are unmistakable that they will find profitability increasingly more elusive in the Information Age.

The MNM Team Building Process is sensitive to accommodating the needs of all stakeholders and presents useful strategies and tactics which you and your team can use effectively for meeting those needs. Specifically, the results and benefits that you can expect to realize for each of your stakeholder groups include:

For the business and its owner:
- Increased productivity
- Improved and more consistent quality
- Increased profits
- More loyal, responsible, and accountable employees
- More motivated employees
- Satisfied customers
- More new customers
- More repeat customers
- Better service and prices from vendors
- Greater enjoyment of profession

For the employees:
- More meaningful work
- A non-stressful work environment
- Opportunity to be self-managing and have greater pride in work
- Opportunity to demonstrate creativity and innovation
- Opportunity for personal growth
- Opportunity for better pay
- Greater job security
- Opportunity to be enthusiastic about work

For the customers and community:
- A more dependable and valuable resource
- Consistent quality and service
- An example of a responsible, ethical business
- A vendor that is interested in their success

For the vendors:
- A stronger, dependable and more stable customer
- A customer that can be trusted to practice win/win philosophy
- An example of successful good business practice
- A customer that inspires better service

Sound useful? Good!

OVERVIEW OF
THE MNM TEAM BUILDING PROCESS

The MNM Team Building Process consists of five separate phases (see also figure 2.1):

Phase I	Developing the Mission and Vision Statements
Phase II	Developing the Preliminary Long-term Strategy
Phase III	Building the Team
Phase IV	On-Going Improvement Work
Phase V	On-Going Strategic Work

The first two phases and the last phase involve only you, the business owner. Phases III and IV are staff meetings and will involve you and all of your staff. They should not be undertaken until Phases I and II are completed.

To illustrate and guide the work you will do in The MNM Process, we have used a case study approach. You will follow one printing company—Best Image Printing—as its owner and staff worked through the five phases of The MNM Team Building Process. Although the company's name is fictitious, the examples and data presented are, for the most part, factual.

This chapter presents an overview of the entire process so that you can understand the general course of action and begin thinking about some of the necessary logistics and requirements.

Phase I   **Developing the Mission and Vision Statements**

Every business, regardless of size, needs *comprehensive* and *meaningful* mission and vision statements. In a very real way, the mission and vision statements of your company are the essence of everything you and your company stand for in business. They convey your purpose, your dreams, your expectations, and state what you will do to attain them. As such, they are absolutely critical.

Figure 2.1

THE MNM TEAM BUILDING PROCESS
IDEAL VISION
MODIFY STRATEGY
MONITOR PROGRESS
FORMALIZE STRATEGY
INCREASED PRODUCTIVITY
IMPROVED QUALITY
MONITOR PROGRESS
THE PATH OF PROGRESS
NEW WORKING METHODS BEGIN TO TAKE EFFECT
WORK ON BUILDING TEAM
TAKE SNAPSHOT IN TIME OF COMPANY
PROCESS IMPLEMENTATION BASELINE
CREATE MISSION & VISION
DEVELOP PRELIMINARY STRATEGY
PRODUCTIVITY & QUALITY BASELINE
PHASE I
PHASE II
PRELIMINARY WORK
OWNER—1-2 WEEKS
PHASE III
TEAM BUILDING WORK
OWNER & STAFF—BI-WEEKLY 2 HR. SESSIONS FOR 12-16 WEEKS
PHASE IV
ON-GOING IMPROVEMENT WORK
OWNER & STAFF—TRI-WEEKLY 2 HR. SESSIONS, ON-GOING
PHASE V
ON-GOING STRATEGIC WORK
OWNER—ONCE A MONTH, ON-GOING
© 1991 MICHAEL P. O'CONNOR

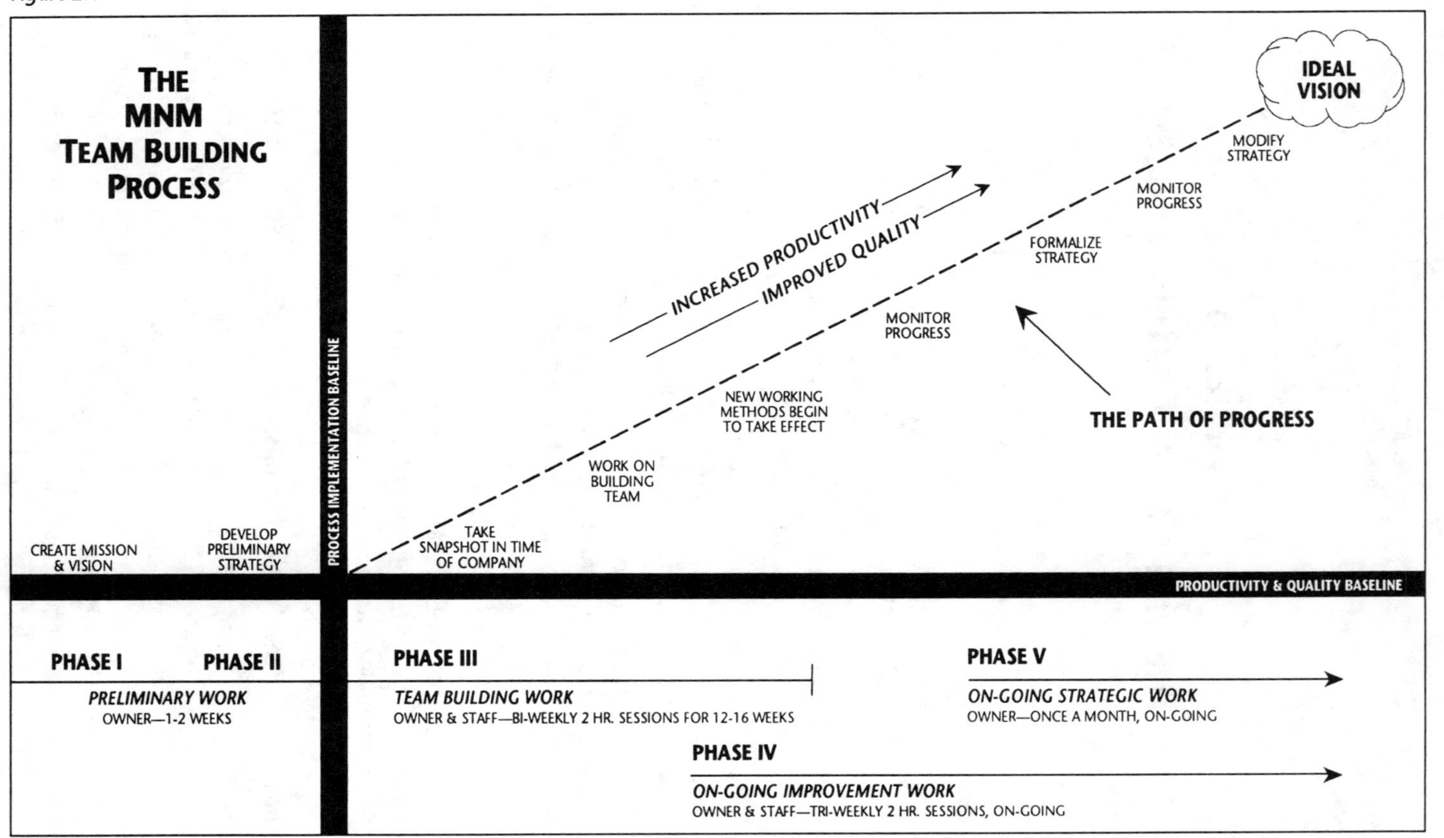

Yet as basic as mission and vision statements might seem, it is really surprising the number of businesses, even very large ones, that either don't have them, or don't use them to advantage, or whose statements are so general or vague that they are virtually useless.

Large companies generally develop mission and vision statements by a group or at least approve one through consensus of a group. As a small business owner, however, this is *your* task and yours alone. In Chapter 4 we will focus first on developing an effective mission statement, one that captures the purpose of your business as you would like it to be. Then in Chapter 5 you will create an overall vision statement of what your business will do to fulfill its mission. Included in this work will be the development of the necessary values and principles for attaining your mission and vision as you perceive them and for guiding company growth and improvement in the future.

Phase II   **Developing the Preliminary Long-Term Strategy**

If the vision statement represents where you see your company heading, it follows that you will need a long-term strategy to guide your journey there. In Chapter 9 we will focus on developing a *preliminary* long-term strategy. This strategy is preliminary in the sense that it will be developed as an outline or skeleton which you will revise and flesh out in Phase V of The MNM Process.

There are two reasons for preparing a preliminary long-term strategy:

1. to focus on critical issues that you, as owner, need to come to terms with before beginning the work of Phases III and IV, and

2. to provide a measuring stick for future use in identifying and evaluating the changes in your own personal perspectives and understanding as you go through the process.

Like Phase I, Phase II is entirely your own work.

Phase III   **Building the Team**

Phase III is the heart of The MNM Process and will require the on-going involvement of you and your staff in a series of 14 two-hour meetings. These meetings will begin with an in-depth analysis of your business as it is today. In this analysis, every facet of your current operation—facilities, equipment, products and services, vendors, customers, competition, marketing and sales, general economic outlook—will be examined in terms of current strengths and weaknesses.

The objective of the Phase III meetings is to produce a *Snapshot In Time* of your existing business system. Then, using this snapshot as a reference and a guide to opportunities for improvement, you and your staff will discover and explore potential new ways of working which will enhance productivity and improve quality.

Towards the end of this phase, not only will productivity and quality be improving, but your staff (and probably yourself as well) will be quite surprised to realize that during this work they have evolved into a high-performance, self-managing team. With this high-performance superteam, you will be able to achieve, refine and exceed the vision of your company's future which you struggled to capture in Phase I.

Most people find the work of Phase III refreshingly stimulating and creative, yet at the same time difficult. Why difficult? The reason is simple: both you and your staff will be involved in *change*. Change in any shape or form is difficult, but change involving the way people work and interrelate with one another is perhaps the most difficult, particularly when those work patterns and relationships have been established over any length of time.

For you as owner, the hardest part of these meetings will be encouraging input from your staff without stifling their creativity or leading their discussions. You will need to accept the risk that comes with letting go. For your staff, their difficulty will be just the opposite; they will be struggling with the risk of accepting responsibility and voicing their thoughts and opinions in your presence.

Chapters 10, 11 and 12 will provide the tools and support necessary to enable you to facilitate your own Phase III staff meetings.

The work of Phase III is spread over a period of several months, at two-week intervals.

Phase IV   **On-Going Improvement Work**

Once the self-managing work team is in place and functioning, the process can focus on ways of assuring continuous improvement and long-term sustainable growth for your company during the months and years ahead. An important function of this phase will be to continue to solicit staff input on various elements of the company's strategy, to encourage team problem solving, and to develop effective strategic monitoring techniques.

One of the reasons so many business improvement strategies fail is that they do not have a built-in system to monitor progress towards the company's vision, particularly progress in areas that are difficult to assess, such as quality improvement and customer response. One of the key points of The MNM Process is that it provides the opportunity for periodic *reality checks* which will help the team take on needed areas of improvement or potential trouble spots in time to implement positive remedial action *before* problems get out of hand. This *team preventive maintenance* will yield benefits over time, but are difficult to appreciate until the system has been implemented for several months.

By this time in the process, the bi-weekly staff meetings will have become a routine and, most likely, anticipated event. One sure sign that the process is taking effect is when you overhear your staff making remarks about how some issue should be taken up at the next meeting. In Chapter 13 we will see how these meetings can be modified to more effectively harness the combined talents and brain power of your staff and sharpen your competitive edge. The chapter will continue the case study approach. Chapter 14 presents a number of useful techniques and concepts that will lead your staff to greater understanding of the creative power and personal satisfaction that comes from being part of a high performance team.

Phase V   **On-Going Strategic Work**

Once Phase IV has started, it's time to begin work on Phase V. In this phase you, the owner, will formalize the long-term strategy you'll use to attain the goals you identified in Phase I.

Like Phases I and II, you will once again be doing the work yourself; this time, however, you're really not working alone as you have several months' combined efforts of your new self-managing team to guide you.

Chapters 15 and 16 will lead you step by step through this phase of the process. It begins by reviewing the work you did in Phases I and II. In all probability, much of that work will now seem deficient and in need of substantial modification and upgrading. This is good and should be expected, because during the past several months not only has your staff been developing into a more productive self-managing team, but *you* have been learning and growing yourself. During this time you will have discovered many things about your staff, your customers, your business, and yourself, and it will be hard to imagine you ever could have considered your efforts for Phases I and II as being complete in any sense of the word. This may be hard to believe now, but that's just the point. It's simply human nature to think that the ideas, thoughts and approaches that we presently utilize could ever be improved upon!

Once the review of Phases I and II is complete, Chapter 16 will focus on revising your long-term strategy so that it will guide your business for the next year or two. Why only one or two years? In part, because in considering the current rate of change that impacts the printing industry, a strategy of longer duration would probably be obsolete before it could be accomplished. But the prime reason is because The MNM Process provides for *constant* monitoring and *continual* improvement of your component visions and their strategies, and consequently, you will frequently be updating your long-term strategy in a cyclical process of on-going improvement. This is not to say that your strategy will be a wishy-washy piece of fluff! Far from it. It will be very complete and very detailed. It will not only provide a short-term action plan and schedule of implementation, but will also include a section on contingency plans in areas of uncertainty.

This, then, is The MNM Team Building Process which you will be experiencing over the next several months. Obviously, it is not a quick-fix process. But for the printshop committed to achieving greater productivity and superior quality, it will work—and the results will be significant, cumulative and sustainable.

Before we begin the process, however, take a few minutes to examine the diagram of the phases of The MNM Team Building Process (figure 2.1).

This diagram summarizes The MNM Process and illustrates the positive changes in productivity and quality that can be expected as your company moves through the five phases of the process. Changes in productivity or quality should begin to show up after Phase III has been in progress for two or three sessions. Unfortunately, the changes will not result in constant improvement. Throughout Phase III, and to a lesser extent throughout the process, the Path of Progress for productivity and quality will be a series of ups *and* downs. Early in the process, it is not uncommon—and, in fact, it should be expected—that productivity and quality may even get *worse*! But don't be alarmed! This is a temporary effect as people become accustomed to working together in new ways. Breaking away from the *status quo* is not easy! Remember: no pain, no gain!

You may find it useful to refer to this diagram often as you work through the process. In fact, you may find it helps to make copies or an overhead transparency of this diagram to use in the meetings you will be facilitating with your staff. Once you've looked over and understand the phases of The MNM Team Building Process, you're ready to begin Phase I.

■

DEVELOPING

THE

MISSION AND VISION

STATEMENTS

CHAPTER 3

MISSION, VISION, AND STRATEGY DEFINED

The MNM Process begins with the objective of developing a strong sense of mission and vision for your company. *The importance of this phase cannot be overemphasized.* For reasons which will become clear as we go along, this work is, in fact, critical to the success of the rest of the process. So, even if you already have a mission statement for your company, please give this chapter your full attention and effort, anyway.

Mission, vision, and strategy are three common words which are often used interchangeably when referring to the long-term direction and focus of effort for a business.

In The MNM Process mission, vision, and strategy take on very specific meanings—meanings which offer important new perspectives on how a company sees itself and the way it is perceived by its stakeholders. (As used in this book, stakeholders refers to all the people who are in any way involved with your company, including yourself, your staff, customers, vendors, and the community.)

The Why, What, and How of Your Business

Recently, a business associate asked me to join him in meeting with a couple of people who, along with a third partner, had just pooled their talents as a new firm offering comprehensive business management services to the community. The purpose of the meeting was networking, that rather obligatory part of American entrepreneurship today which says that if you know what everybody else does and they all know what you do, then surely it will lead to more business. In any case, the meeting was fairly long, with each of the four of us taking a turn at carefully explaining *what* it was that we did. When we each had finished, there came a rather awkward pause before a few comments were offered as to how we could probably refer clients to one another (except for me; I was a problem, they said, because their other partner already did what I did). Then came another pause in which no one seemed to know what to say. After a few minutes of this I ventured, "Well, now that we all know *what* we do, there's another whole area that we might share and that's *why* we do what we do." Silence. Finally, one of the people turned to me and in a puzzled voice said, "You know, that *is* an interesting question. I don't think I've ever really thought much about that before."

If you think about it, most of us are quite good at expounding on *what* we do or are going to do in our profession or business. Likewise, we generally have little difficulty in telling *how* we do it. *Why* we do it is another matter, and for most people it *is* a more difficult question. Yet it is an important question. Many successful business owners would argue it is the *most* important question. Yogi Berra once said something to the effect that if you don't know where you're going, you might end up somewhere else. To paraphrase Yogi, and drive home the importance of this concept, perhaps we could just leave it by saying that if you don't know *why* you are in business, then soon you may not be there.

Mission, vision, and strategy can be considered the why, what and how of your business. The focus of Chapters 4 and 5 is to help you consider and articulate as clearly as possible the mission and vision of your business. In

Figure 3.1

**DEFINITIONS OF MISSION, VISION, AND STRATEGY
AS USED IN THE MNM PROCESS**

MISSION	The *special purpose* or function of your business—in essence, its reason for being. Must consider and involve *all stakeholders*. Based on and may express *guiding principles, values, or concepts*. Generally *remains unchanging* through time.
VISION	The ideal mental *image* of *what your business does or will do* in the future to fulfill its mission. Includes *all aspects* of your business—its products, services, facilities, personnel, etc., as well as your customers, vendors, markets and the way they fit together to form *the big picture* of where you see your business heading. Can be considered in terms of an *overall general vision consisting of several parts*, or smaller visions. Must be in *total alignment with the mission*. Generally will *change* through time.
STRATEGY	The devised *plan of action* which you systematically implement to achieve your vision. Must be in *total alignment with the mission*. Is *constantly monitored* for effectiveness. Generally *changes frequently* through time.

Chapter 6 we'll start working on strategy. But just to make sure we're together in our thinking, look a little closer at the definitions in figure 3.1.

Some Examples of Mission, Vision, and Strategy

Hopefully, you now understand the meaning of mission, vision and strategy as used in The MNM Process. In the next two chapters we will use this understanding to develop mission and vision statements for your business. But before we do, you might find it useful to look at figure 3.2 (on the next page) which offers examples of mission, vision, and strategy for different types of businesses. Each of the examples given contains most of the elements we have been discussing, and as you can readily see, the concepts can be applied to virtually any kind of business or organization.

Figure 3.2 ■ **EXAMPLES OF MISSION, VISION, AND STRATEGY**

BUSINESS	MISSION	VISION	STRATEGY
BUILD-RITE LUMBER CO.	To be the most knowledgeable and reliable source of wood construction materials within our community.	Offer a wide selection of domestic and imported dimensional lumber and prefabricated wood products. Serve both contractors and general public. Free delivery within 50 mile radius. Cross-trained staff with individual specialties.	Have close personal working relationships with suppliers, computerized inventory, and just-in-time delivery for contractors. Provide continual staff training in products. Offer monthly classes in do-it-yourself maintenance for homeowners.
SERVICE TAXI COMPANY	Perfection in hassle-free transportation!	Fleet of dependable new cars operated by courteous, company-trained drivers. Dependable scheduling and instant response capability.	State-of-the-art company repair shop. Company training programs include both driving and customer service skills. On-line computer scheduling/dispatcher capability with real-time unit location monitoring utilizing GPS technology.
AN APPLE A DAY, INC.	To create a healthier, happier world through the magic of the apple!	A family orchard specializing in apples of Early Americana. A farm outlet/catalog store with all types of apple related items, including fresh fruit, processed products, recipe books, seedlings, orchard tools, etc.	Create a local tourist attraction which includes the opportunity to tour the orchard, processing plant, and farm outlet store, along with follow-up mail order. Every facet of operation will in some way celebrate the multitudinous benefits of the apple.
BEST IMAGE PRINTING	To help people market their products, their services, and themselves through the use of printed materials, and to serve in any way we can, even if it means referring the customer elsewhere.	A multi-service printing firm, offering offset printing, high speed copying, color copying, typesetting and design, bindery, and support services. We will serve all sizes of business, as well as the private sector, with a focus on quality, and will strive to make every customer a repeat customer.	To nurture our market niche by expanding our existing capabilities, particularly in color printing and high speed copying; by retaining, expanding and recession-proofing our customer base; by building the staff into a self-managing team; and by developing reliable and dependable vendors.

CHAPTER 4

THE MISSION STATEMENT

Several years ago, I was relaxing over dinner with an associate who had been president of a major U.S. food products company. The company had been a family-owned business for three generations and was, by anyone's standards, the consummate American success story. Emerging from humble beginnings in his grandparents garage in New York, the company had grown steadily through the years until its quality products were being savored in homes throughout the eastern half of the country. Ultimately, the family sold the business to a giant multinational corporation.

As we sat there talking, my thoughts turned to an embroidered plaque which I had seen prominently displayed on the wall above my associate's desk. The plaque was quite small and had only six words neatly stitched on a field of white: *When In Doubt, Do What's Right.*

Now this was a man who valued his privacy, but I was curious and enquired as to the plaque's significance. "Oh," he said, "that's our company motto; my wife embroidered it for me." Intrigued, I proceeded to pursue the matter. "How did you come by it?", I asked. "My father. He ran the business by it, too." "Really! Do you know where he got it?", I pressed. "From my grandfather, I guess," was the reply, "I think he brought it with him from the old country." The story fascinated me. "Do you mean to tell me, then, that these six words—When In Doubt, Do What's Right—are the words which have been responsible for the success of your family's business for three generations?", I asked incredulously. "Well, yes, I suppose you could put it that way," he responded somewhat pensively. He then went on to explain at some length how those little words had served as a touchstone down through the years, guiding the countless choices that the company had made, from major decisions to small, from the selection of distributors to the selection of the quality ingredients for which their products had become famous.

The dinner came to an end. I thanked my associate profusely for sharing this wonderful story with me, as I truly found it inspiring. There was still one

---

question, though, I felt I had to ask, and somewhat hesitatingly, I told him so. "Sure," he said, "fire away!" "Well," I said, thinking that it was a dumb question, "how do you know what *is* the right thing to do?" Upon hearing my words, he threw back his head and laughed. "Oh, that's easy," he grinned, "everybody *knows* what's the right thing to do; the problem is they just don't *do* it!"

When In Doubt, Do What's Right—the ultimate mission statement? For this business it was. Six words to successfully guide a major company for three generations! Amazing.

Some Do, But Many Don't ...

Unfortunately, many businesses don't have such a consistent understanding of mission. Not too long ago, I was engaged in a consulting project for a university which involved on-site assessment of the training needs for a variety of small businesses. The purpose of the project was to gather relevant information from both management and employees which could be used to help guide curriculum development. The first part of these participatory workshops focused on providing background on the mission, products and general nature of the business; the second part went on to explore current and future plans and projected training needs.

When I began synthesizing the data, I remember how surprised I was at how unclear many of the participants were when it came to answering the questions concerning the mission statement, such as did the company have one, how did employees find out about it, was there a mechanism for periodic review, and so on. Quite a number of the employees said they had never seen one. At one company I learned that a mission statement had been developed several years ago but was kept by the president and senior management and not made available to general employees! When asked to write a short, appropriate mission statement for their business, again the results were rather vague, generally consisting of generic descriptions of the products and services that the company offered. Ultimately I discovered that *one-third* of the businesses participating in the assessment did not have a formal mission statement.

Of course, this was not true of all the businesses. Some were very clear as to their company's mission and could articulate it well. In looking back, I now understand that such ambiguity concerning company mission is rather typical. However, that is not to say that it is healthy. Quite to the contrary. The more one looks into it, the more one learns that companies which repeatedly give a strong, innovative and successful performance are companies which also have a strong and clear sense of mission and vision.

Your Mission Has a *Special Purpose*

Each of us is a unique individual, the sum of all our inherited gifts, education, and experiences. And as such, each of us has a special purpose or potential contribution to make to the world in general, and to our profession. No one should or could run his or her business exactly like you. And no business should be exactly like yours. Unfortunately, this is not always the case as all too often our uniqueness does not—or is not allowed to—shine through in our work. Today, businesses, like the people who run them, tend to be to driven by external factors which mask their uniqueness. Call it the "mall syndrome" or the "fast-food syndrome," the result is all too often the same: homogeneous, bland and … boring. Initially, many of these businesses *were* unique, which is what led to their success, and also to their reproduction, endlessly, until all the specialness and uniqueness was lost.

Think for a moment. If you were asked to describe your all-time favorite sandwich shop, what would it be? Is it or was it special? Unique? You bet it was. Was it successful? You bet it was. Could they hold their own against the *big boys*? Did the owner's special light come through? The point of all of this is that one of the most important factors in defining your mission is the specialness of your endeavor. What is it that sets your business apart from the rest of the competition? What is it that puts the *you* in the business? Ben and Jerry found it; so did Donald Burr in Peoples Express. And so did the owner of your favorite sandwich shop.

Your Mission as a Joint Venture
Which Includes *All the Stakeholders*

Many people, when asked why they are in business, will quickly respond, "Why, to make money, of course!" Let's consider that response for a moment. Certainly there's no question that making money is the bottom line of any successful business. But is making money the *why* of a successful business? Is it the ultimate mission? Or it is, ultimately, just one of the positive *results*?

Recently, Marsha Sinetar wrote a well-received book titled *Do What You Love, the Money Will Follow*. Sinetar's message is clear and simple: when a person is engaged in activity which is in alignment with what that person really holds important, then success and the money that accompanies it comes quite naturally and abundantly. There are lots of well-documented stories which support this idea. You probably can think of quite a few yourself.

Now, if we look a little closer at the relationship between doing what you love and doing to make money, something rather interesting emerges relative to this concept of mission. Namely, people can become *very* interested in why you love doing what you do even though they might not, at the time, share a need for your product or service themselves. They can be interested because what they see is your enthusiasm, wonder, creativity— essentially, your excitement about life itself! Now, how interested are the same people in hearing about *why* you want to make a lot of money? Not very. Unless, if we want to be cynical, they think they can make some, too! No, money is not a part of mission. A result, definitely. A goal, perhaps, unless it becomes obsessive. But, it is *not* a mission.

On the other hand, doing what you love, it seems, *could* be an important part of mission. Why? What is the difference here? Aren't we really talking about personal goals and objectives, whether we are talking about doing what we love or doing to make a lot of money? Yes, but there is an important fundamental difference. Love always involves sharing—money does not. To do what you love in business is to be *connected to your stakeholders by sharing*. When you do what you love, you are sharing the essence of yourself, that special purpose we already talked about. Another way of putting it is that your mission can be considered a joint venture—a joint venture of *alignment* and *purpose*. And, like any joint venture, your sense of mission must consider all of your partners if it is to be successful.

Lest you think we are getting too philosophical here, think for a moment about the sales representative that you most enjoy doing business with. Now think about the one that you wish would transfer to another state. How do you perceive *their* sense of mission?

Your Mission as a *Declaration of Principles and Values*

Principles and values are making a comeback. Maybe not everywhere, certainly, and not in every business. But it *is* happening and the momentum is building. The cynics would say that it's too little too late; the optimists would say it's better late than never. But, hopefully, just maybe, the aberrant strain within our society that has spawned the S & L crises, the junk bond scams, and the Love Canals is beginning to weaken. Perhaps our "nation of independent operators" (a phrase I came across in a weekly news magazine) is beginning to come back to some basics, particularly the notion that individual success is really a measure of our connectedness to others.

One might ask what happened to our values and principles in the first place? Where did they go and where have they been? Nowhere, really. It's just that they have been ignored, tabled and denied in our collective rush to participate in the Deal-of-the-Month and Independent-Operator-of-the-Year competitions. But this is changing. From Ford, where Quality has *again* become Number 1, to ethics courses in the MBA program at Harvard, there is a fresh scent in the air.

Why the change? Many reasons: the further maturing of our society, a growing collective awareness of the limits of our global resources, a shift from short-term to long-term perspective, increasing personal understanding that as individuals we are accountable and responsible. All of these things and lots more. But relative to our discussion of mission there is a rather simple and pragmatic reason why values and principles are increasingly being reinstated as key issues: the spreading awareness that they lead to *sustained profitability.* This is nothing new, because if you stop and think for a moment, the businesses which have continued to be successful down through the years never really lost sight of that fact.

So, what kind of values and principles are best? Again, that's *your* choice. I know one company that absolutely thrives on "The Golden Rule." "Doing What's Right" seems to be a winner, too. The important thing to keep in mind is, implicit or explicit, it's not how you *say* it, it's how you *live* it!

Your Mission as *Unchanging*

Do people really change that much in their lifetime? Or is it that we just become more skillful or focused in living that special purpose we talked about? What is the relationship of your personal mission to your company's mission? Unless there is more than one owner involved, the chances are that they are pretty much the same. If you are doing what you love, how could they be much different? Again, if you stop and think about it, isn't this one of the prime reasons for going into business for yourself, to have a business where you can daily express yourself, your creativity, your values, rather than the schizoid life of trying to live someone else's mission by day and your own by night?

So for most of us and for our businesses, missions *are* unchanging. Such *consistency of purpose* is not only reassuring to our customers and other stakeholders, but *valued* as well. Surely you have had at one time or another the experience where a favorite store or company changed its mission to one which no longer included *you*. Probably you went through a period of time where you tried to adjust to this new mission by making excuses for their lack of purpose, only to eventually drift away. Companies with good, consistent missions are much like good friends—hard to find.

CHAPTER 5

THE VISION STATEMENT

My long-time friend Charlie was fond of saying, "What the mind can conceive, the body can achieve." And since Charlie and I were involved in business together, I got to hear it *often*! Charlie was a classic good ol' southern optimist and had evolved his own home-grown formula for success in business: just create in your mind the picture of what you want your business to be, then work hard, and after a while you'll get it! I remember travelling with him on long business trips where he would go on and on describing in great detail and clarity what our fledgling business would become—the new plant, the international markets, the exciting new products. Whenever I lapsed into the realities of the way things were going at the time, out it would come again, *What the mind can conceive ...*

Looking back, Charlie's understanding of vision was right on the mark. Maintaining clarity as to the *ideal image* of what your business does and will do in the future is absolutely critical to the success of the venture. But, as we will explore in the following pages, creating the detailed vision is only a *first* step.

Seeing the Big Picture *and* the Details of Your Vision *Simultaneously*

Traditionally, large company CEOs have been given the primary responsibility of keeping track of the *big picture,* leaving lower management the task of *working out the details.* Such duality in management and planning can be successful, providing there is good communication in the organization, but such a system is susceptible to serious dysfunction when there is not.

In later chapters we will look at some concepts of management which eliminate these and other problems by encouraging involvement of company staff in all phases of the visioning process. For now, however, the point is that as the owner of a small printshop, you have ultimate responsibility for maintaining clarity in vision for *both* the big picture and the smaller visions *simultaneously*. The fact that you perceive an opportunity in an apparent industry trend towards increased color printing is not enough, you must also be able to translate this overall vision into various component visions for your company, such as facilities, equipment, personnel, and customer base.

Your Overall Vision Comes from the *Component Visions*

The fact is that while you need an overall vision of what your company will do to achieve its mission, your day-to-day efforts always focus on the individual component parts of your business, such as customers, equipment, marketing, etc. So before you can develop your overall vision, you must first develop a vision for each of the component parts. These component visions will be general in nature (specifics will come later when you develop your preliminary strategies) and must be compatible with each other. Once they have been developed, it will be easy to synthesize them into one overall vision.

Aligning the Vision with the Mission

In creating your vision, be it the overall vision or the component visions, it's important that there be close alignment with the mission. In a real sense, the degree of alignment between vision and mission provides a sensitive indicator as to the overall health of a company. Unfortunately, both in times of stress and of plenty, companies can lose sight of this fact and either through panic or neglect, resort to *alternate visions of expediency*. Such diversions from mission rarely work, and for the most part are counterproductive.

Probably all of us at one time or another have witnessed the unfortunate situation of a well-established company that loses sight of its mission and begins to flounder, jumping from one poorly conceived vision to the next. In such situations customers become very sensitive to this loss of alignment, and once customers' confidence is shaken, it can be extremely difficult to regain.

While it is true that a company's mission is often rather general and somewhat abstract, not so with the vision. Visions are very concrete and tangible. Implementation of your company vision should be, in fact, the day-to-day manifestation of your company's mission. Periodic reality checks of your company's vision with the mission are one more form of preventive medicine to ensure the sustained health of your company.

Allow Your Vision the Freedom to *Change Frequently*

The human tendency to stay with a successful method, product or idea once it is perfected is incredibly strong. In days past, such consistency in business could be counted on to yield repetitive positive results—a definite asset. Today it is a definite liability. Unlike your mission, which tends to remain unchanged through time, you should expect that your vision (what you do to fulfill that mission) *will change frequently.*

As stressed earlier, the ability of a printing business to be flexible, innovative and responsive to the changing needs and demands of its customers will increasingly determine the sustainability of that company's success. Accordingly, your business strategy must include a mechanism for monitoring your vision and then provide a system for implementing change *when it is necessary.* The key, of course, is the *when* part. In a service business like printing, change for the sake of change is not advisable. Indeed, *unnecessary change can be as detrimental as resistance to change.*

One of the key elements of The MNM Process is the provision for periodic monitoring of the vision to identify and facilitate needed change. We will take a *detailed* look at this part of the process in Chapters 13 through 16.

CHAPTER 6

CREATING YOUR COMPANY'S MISSION STATEMENT

The time has come to begin the applied approach to The MNM Process (that means it's time to go to work!). Chapters 6 and 7 will guide you as you develop a clear, written statement of your company's mission and vision. Perhaps you may have already developed such statements for your business. If so, you are asked to set them aside for the time being and give full effort to doing the exercises presented here. Chances are the statements you write now, having read the previous chapters, will be substantially different.

Take a little break from reading, get yourself a pad and pencil and a cup of coffee, and get ready to do some thoughtful and reflective work (which you should find enjoyable). Find yourself a quiet place where you won't be disturbed for an hour or so and begin working.

Developing the Company Mission Statement

Part 1: Two Conversations About Mission

A. DIALOGUE WITH YOUR BEST FRIEND AND TEACHER

Each of us has had at least one special person in our life who was not only an excellent teacher or mentor, but was also a really good friend. This person might be from your formal education years, or could be someone from the business world or some other part of your life experience. Close your eyes and think for a moment to identify this person. The identity of the individual is not as important as your relationship to the person, who should be someone for whom you had great respect and in whom you felt totally free to share your innermost thoughts, without fear of harsh judgement or ridicule. This person could always be counted on to listen carefully to your latest plans and to help you see the issues more clearly. Continue on when you have the person in mind.

Now, imagine for the moment that your friend, who you haven't seen for years, is passing through town and suggests you have dinner together to talk over old times. You agree and meet at your favorite restaurant. Eventually the conversation gets around to your present printing business and to what you are doing professionally. Your friend listens carefully as you ramble on enthusiastically for some time about how you got into the business, the kinds of printing work you do, and business in general. Then your friend leans forward, smiles and says, "Hey, that's really great! Sounds like you have a really challenging opportunity. But, you know, you still haven't told me the best part yet!" "What's that?", you ask. "Well, you know … *why* you're doing it, what your purpose is for being in this business, and what it is that makes your business so special." You smile, and as you begin to ponder these questions, think, "isn't that so typical … hard questions, as always!" You take a couple of minutes to make some notes on your napkin and then after a few minutes silence (you let the suspense build, knowing that your mentor is really anticipating your response), you begin, "Well, I guess there are one or two major reasons."

In the space below, or on your pad, write down what you shared with your friend. (And don't forget to consider all the stakeholders and those values and principles that you think are so important.)

Well, the special purpose of my business is :

____

____

____

But, then, some of the other reasons would be:

____

____

____

Guiding principles or values? Well, I suppose they would be:

____

____

____

____

____

Eventually, your friend seems satisfied that you indeed have a mission and you finish off the evening with a great desert. You return home pleased, but thinking what an odd experience that was.

B. DIALOGUE WITH YOUR NEIGHBOR'S TEN-YEAR-OLD

The next day, returning from work, you encounter your neighbor's ten-year-old in the yard. The child is really bright and in the past you have enjoyed your conversations together. "I need to ask you some questions," the child begins. "It's part of our homework; our teacher is having us do a report on what business is all about." "Oh," you say, not really believing what you're hearing, particularly after your dinner last night, "well, sure, what do you want to know." "Well, our teacher says that businesses are sort of like people and that every business should have a special purpose or missile or something." "Do you mean mission?", you offer, still not believing what you're hearing. "Yeah! Mission. So can you tell me about the mission of your printing business?" The child seems really pleased and blurts out, "I knew you'd know!" (Flattery always works, especially from children.) In a flash of inspiration you pull out the napkin with your notes from last night and launch into an eloquent speech on the mission of your company. Five minutes later you finish, feeling very smug that you could have pulled this off so easily. Unfortunately, the child is not impressed, and says, "You know, I didn't understand anything you said. It sure *sounds* like you know what your business is about, but can't you put it into kid's language—you know, everyday little words for little people?" "Little words for little people," you muse. Perplexed, you think for a moment, look over your napkin again and then proceed to translate your big thoughts into ordinary language that a ten-year-old could easily understand.

In the space below or on your pad, write down what you finally come up with to tell your little friend.

Well, in little words that everyone should be able to understand, the special purpose of my business is:

____

____

____

And, some of the other big reasons why I'm in business are:

____

____

____

____

Finally, the things that help guide me to do the right thing are:

____

____

____

____

Part 2: Creating Your Mission Statement

In looking over the notes from your two discussions, you should now be able to write a comprehensive and meaningful mission statement for your business. The idea, of course, is to be able to combine your thoughts from these two dialogues into one concise and meaningful statement which clearly sets out, for all to quickly understand, what the mission of your business is really all about. Ideally, your finished product will combine the wisdom and insight of your deepest and best thoughts with the simplicity and lucidity of the language of the child.

BEST IMAGE PRINTING'S MISSION STATEMENT

The mission of Best Image Printing is to help people market their products, their services, and themselves through the use of printed materials, and to serve in any way we can, even if it means referring the customer elsewhere.

What To Do with Your Mission Statement

Now that you've got your new mission statement, an obvious question is what do you do with it. Once you have it typed and are reasonably satisfied, the best thing to do for now is to put it away. After a few days you can give it a final editing.

This is a good point to start a binder in which you can keep MNM Process minutes and documents. Your new mission statement will be the first entry.

Once you are satisfied with the final content and wording of your new mission statement, put it to use! Here are a few suggestions; we're sure you can come up with others.

- Typeset it, frame it, and hang it in your reception area
- Use it in your yellow pages ad
- Design a direct mail piece around it

CREATING YOUR COMPANY'S VISION STATEMENT

It is quite possible that you found the work you did in Chapter 6 difficult. If so, don't feel you're alone. For many people, coming up with the *right* mission statement can be a real challenge. In any case, you'll probably find that developing your vision statement is much easier.

The objective of Chapter 7 is to develop an *overall* ideal vision of what you desire your business to be in the long-term* future, specifically the next one to two years. To achieve this comprehensive vision, however, it is easier to begin by considering the ideal vision for the component parts.

The overall ideal vision of every business can be broken down into various constituent parts. Some of the component parts of a printing business include:

- products and services
- customer base
- physical facilities
- equipment
- staff
- vendors
- marketing and sales
- competition

While general, the above list is a good starting point for developing the component visions that will ultimately combine to become the overall ideal vision of what you want your company to be like in 12 to 18 months. Remember to keep these component visions non-specific. The strategies you

---

* Throughout this book the terms "long-term" and "short-term" are used extensively. Our definition of long-term is 12 to 18 months. Short-term would, then, be anything less than 12 months. We feel that due to the constant change in printing industry technology, it's impossible to realistically plan beyond 18 months.

Figure 7.1 ■ **PRODUCTS & SERVICES VISION WORKSHEET** / Best Image Printing

PRESENT PRODUCT/SERVICE	PROPOSED PRODUCT/SERVICE	PRESENT/PROPOSED % OF SALES		POTENTIAL CUSTOMERS	ADDITIONAL SPACE NEEDED	EQUIPMENT NEEDED	STAFF NEEDED
Single and multi color offset printing	Increase capacity for color printing	70	50	All types—business, general public, education	150 sq. ft.	New two-color offset press	Trainee press operator from technical school to take over single-color press
High speed copying	Increase capacity	10	20	Primarily business—particularly legal, manufacturing and financial	100 sq. ft.	High speed copier	None
	Color copying	0	5	All types—business and general public	None	Color copier	None
Buyouts	No change	5	10	All types	None	None	None
Typesetting and design	Integrate with color computer	10	10	All types—primarily business	None	Computer with color capability	None
Bindery	Increase capacity	10	10	All types—primarily business	None	New cutter	One half-time person available on short notice

develop later in Phase II will define the specifics of the visions you develop here.

In the following sections you will explore each of these categories by combining your goals and desires with your best crystal ball projections based on current trends in the printing industry. These exercises should be taken very seriously and given your best thought and effort because much of what you are mapping out here is, most likely, what your business *will be* one or two years from now. Certainly, these visions will change as time goes on, but for now they provide the initial compass course to guide the first leg of your journey in The MNM Process.

We suggest that you use the outline and suggested formats provided in this chapter and carefully write out complete descriptions for each of your visions. When completed, each of these descriptions should be typed and put into your binder for future use and reference.

Creating a Preliminary Vision for Your Products and Services

We start with the development of your vision for products and services because of their impact on the other parts of your business. By using the guidelines listed below, along with the worksheet Best Image Printing developed (shown in figure 7.1), you should be able to quickly develop a long-term vision for your products and services.

1. List the products and services you presently offer.

2. Considering your own desires *and* perceived current trends in the industry, list the products and services that you visualize your business offering 12 months from now.

3. Now list and estimate your *present* and *proposed percentage of sales* for each of these products and services.

4. List the types of *customers* you think would be most likely to use these products and services.

5. List additions or changes needed in your *physical facilities* in order to produce the products and services.

6. List *equipment* needed to produce each of the products and services.

7. List additions or changes in *staff* needed to produce each of the products and services.

Once you have completed the above steps, you should summarize the completed format by writing a long-term vision statement for your business'

Figure 7.2 ■ **IDEAL CUSTOMER BASE VISION WORKSHEET** / Best Image Printing

CUSTOMER	TYPE OF BUSINESS	% OF TOTAL SALES (PAST 12 MOS.)	PAYMENT HISTORY	EASE OF SATISFYING CUSTOMER	SATISFACTION FROM SERVING CUSTOMER	ALIGNMENT WITH MISSION	DESIRE FOR GETTING SIMILAR CUSTS.	POTENTIAL FOR GETTING SIMILAR CUSTS.	CUST. RANKING (add A to G)
		A	B	C	D	E	F	G	
Precision Engineering	engineering firm	5	8	2	5	10	5	2	37
Happy Gourmet	retail foods	1	10	8	9	10	10	8	55
Mondo Condo	real estate developer	2	3	8	2	3	3	–	21
Mid-Coast University	small 4-year university	8	6	8	10	10	10	5	57
Good Views	mfgr. of vision products	7	8	9	8	8	10	5	55
Corner Gallery	art gallery	1	1	3	3	5	3	–	16
HiTech Electronics	computer parts manufacturer	4	9	3	8	10	10	5	45
NASRA	trade assn.	2	10	10	10	10	10	5	57

SCALE (see text): 1 = lowest or worst
2 = average
3 = highest or best

IDEAL CUSTOMER RANKING INDEX: Greater than 50 = Ideal Customer! Find more!
30 to 50 = Average Customer
Less than 30 = Problematic Customer. Replace if possible.

products and services.

Best Image Printing
Preliminary Vision for Products and Services

- *Continue to expand printing capabilities into multicolor products, including brochures, stationary, business cards, newsletters, flyers, business forms, small booklets, announcements, and other specialty printing*

- *Expand our capability for high-speed copying for the business sector and continue to research copier technology*

- *Explore ways of incorporating the new color imaging technology into the products and services we offer*

- *Expand our bindery capability to take on larger jobs*

Creating a Preliminary Vision for Your Ideal Customer Base

One does not have to be in business very long before it becomes obvious that not all customers are equal. Some are very loyal, steady customers who pay their bills on time, and over a year's time will be considered a major asset to your business. Others are just the opposite, and over a period of time, when you consider the business that they bring you relative to the time and aggravation spent in serving them, they can actually be considered a liability. While it is perhaps impossible to ever develop a 100% ideal customer base, there is much you can do to direct the growth of your business to where you can spend more of your time dealing with the kinds of customers that bring you the greatest personal satisfaction (as well as greatest profitability) ... a customer base that is in alignment with your mission.

It order to clarify your vision of what you would like your customer base to be a year from now, it is useful to begin by considering your current customer base. Best Image Printing did just that in figure 7.2. Use the guidelines below to develop your own worksheet. When you're done, you should have greater insight into who are your ideal customers.

1. Customer: It's not necessary to include *every* customer you have, but it is important that the list be *representative*, both in terms of businesses and volume. Probably 5% of your charging customers is adequate, along with one or two COD customers; small and large customers should be included.

2. Customer's type of business

3. % of Total Sales (past 12 months): For businesses comprising up to

10% of your gross sales put down actual percentage number. For single customers making up more than 10% of your gross sales, deduct 2 points for each percentage point over 10; (i.e., a customer making up 18% of your gross sales would be ranked -6). The reason for this is, of course, that businesses incur great vulnerability when they become dependent on a single customer for more than 10% of their gross sales.

4. Payment History: Use the following 1-10 scale for ranking:
    1 = pays only after maximum hassle and threats
    5 = generally meets your company's terms
    10 = pays cash, regardless of size of order or always pays within terms

5. Ease of Satisfying Customer: Use the following 1-10 scale:
    1 = extremely difficult to please, requires maximum time and effort
    5 = average time and effort
    10 = very easy to please, very little time or effort

6. Satisfaction from Serving Customer: Use the following 1-10 scale:
    1 = none, very difficult to deal with, leaves shop in turmoil
    5 = average
    10 = maximum, leaves everyone in shop in a good mood

7. Alignment with Mission: Use the following 1-10 scale:
    1 = none, actually conflicts
    5 = no apparent conflict
    10 = total, actually nurtures and expands sense of mission

8. Desirability of Getting Similar Customers: Use the following 1-10 scale:
    1 = absolutely none!
    5 = no problem, but wouldn't actively seek
    10 = highly desirable, should actively seek

9. Potential of Getting Similar Customers: Use the following 1-10 scale *only for those customers ranking 5-10 in desirability:*
    1 = not very likely
    5 = possible
    10 = highly probable

10. Ideal Customer Ranking: Add the rankings in columns A through G to get Ideal Customer Ranking Index. Possible range is from 6 to 70.

Once you have completed the format for a representative sampling of your customers, examine the Ideal Customer Ranking Index of each relative to type of business and percentage of sales. Obviously, these rankings are rather subjective; however, using the three categories below provides a useful evaluation tool.

Greater than 50	=	Ideal customer, find more!
30 - 50	=	Average customer
Less than 30	=	Problematic customer, replace if possible

You can use your results in later sessions with your staff. Our purpose at this time is to use the information to enable you to write a meaningful vision statement for the ideal customer base you would like to have a year from now. Obviously, your statement will represent a composite of several of your better customers.

Most likely, *all* of your customers will never meet your vision of ideal customers, but that doesn't mean you shouldn't keep striving for that vision!

Best Image Printing
Preliminary Vision for Ideal Customer Base

— *Expand our existing customer base by 20% with new customers who comprise a cross section of businesses which would offer least vulnerability to recession*

— *Develop customers who:*

    a)   offer significant repeat business
    b)   are good credit risks
    c)   are relatively easy to satisfy
    d)   are enjoyable to work with
    e)   are in alignment with our mission

(Examples of current customers who exemplify these characteristics would be the Happy Gourmet, Mid-Coast University, Good Views, HiTech Electronics, and NASRA)

Creating a Preliminary Vision for Your Physical Facilities

Creating a long-term vision of what you would like your physical facilities to be can be easily accomplished by turning back to the worksheet you developed for your vision of products and services (figure 7.1). Using these thoughts and projections as a starting point, you should now write a concise, yet specific, vision statement for physical facilities.

Best Image Printing
Preliminary Vision for Physical Facilities

— *Expand space as needed to accommodate growth*

— *Continually monitor and upgrade interior of shop so that it always presents a pleasing image to customers*

Creating a Preliminary Vision for Your Equipment

Creating your long-term vision for equipment can be facilitated by utilizing the worksheet you previously developed for your vision of products and services (figure 7.1). Again, using these thoughts and projections, along with other ideas you might have, write your vision statement for equipment.

Best Image Printing
Preliminary Vision for Equipment

- *On-going investigation of new equipment that will enable us to increase the products and services we offer, incorporate new technology as it becomes available, become more efficient, and remain competitive in our market*

- *Develop a preventive maintenance schedule for each piece of major equipment and a contingency plan for handling breakdowns of critical units*

Creating a Preliminary Vision for Your Staff

The purpose of this exercise is to develop a long-term vision for your staff. In the worksheet you developed for your vision of products and services (figure 7.1) you generated some information regarding necessary new staff. When writing your vision for staff, you will also want to address current staff and related issues, such as training, management, incentives, production, quality standards, etc.

Best Image Printing
Preliminary Vision for Staff

- *Add staff as needed to accommodate growth*

- *Develop a self-managing work team for all staff members to increase productivity and improve quality, and develop more responsible people*

- *Develop an on-going training program utilizing internal and external resources and cross-training to increase skills of all personnel*

- *Develop a new incentive program to encourage increased personal initiative and responsibility*

Creating a Preliminary Vision for Your Vendors

Vendors are the lifeline of any business. Unfortunately, printshops in many areas simply do not have the buying power to encourage the pricing and service that very large commercial printers enjoy. Consequently, it's advantageous to include a section in your vision devoted to vendors. With these thoughts in mind, you should write a long-term vision for vendors which will take positive action on problems you may have experienced in the past.

Best Image Printing
Preliminary Vision for Vendors

- *Improve all sources of supply*

- *Develop stronger personal relationships with existing vendors at the management level as well as at the sales level*

- *Investigate and implement a system of combining many small orders into one larger order to increase your buying power and obtain more competitive pricing*

Creating a Preliminary Vision for Marketing and Sales

The worksheet you developed while working on the vision for your ideal customer base should provide a good starting point for developing your long-term vision for marketing and sales.

Best Image Printing
Preliminary Vision for Marketing and Sales

- *Increase gross sales through introduction of our services to 100 potential new customers*

- *Prepare direct mail pieces that promote our products and services; mail these pieces on a regular basis, without fail*

- *Join area business and civic organizations, and participate on a committee in each one*

- *Perform sales calls as needed*

- *Make sure customers know **everything** we can do*

Creating a Preliminary Vision for Competition

The MNM Process is a process of *on-going* improvement and innovation, in which the goal is to improve the productivity and the quality of your printing business to the extent that you become the standard for printing excellence within your community. Competition is *not* a major focus of The MNM Process, because when a business commits itself to the principles of on-going improvement and innovation, there isn't as great a need for *keeping up with the competition*. Instead, the business is constantly aligned with the wants and needs of the marketplace and its customers. This doesn't mean that you ignore the competition; it simply means that there is no need to be obsessed by it.

In this exercise you are asked to develop a long-term vision statement for your competition.

Best Image Printing
Preliminary Vision for Competition

- _Understand the pricing systems of all other printing shops in the area_
- _Understand the printing capabilities, products and services offered by the other shops_
- _Learn what customers like and dislike about the other shops_
- _Develop a personal relationship with those shops which have complementary services and products and which share a similar business philosophy_

The _Overall_ Ideal Vision Statement for Your Company

Once you have developed your component vision statements, you should have a clear vision of what you would like your business to be like in 12 to 18 months. The next step in Phase I is to summarize these eight component visions into one statement that becomes the _overall_ ideal vision of your company.

Based on their component visions, the owner of Best Image Printing developed the following overall vision statement:

BEST IMAGE PRINTING'S VISION STATEMENT

The overall ideal vision of Best Image Printing is to be a multi-service printing business, offering offset printing, high speed copying, color copying, typesetting and design, bindery, and support services. We will serve all sizes of business, as well as the private sector, with a focus on quality, and will strive to make every customer a repeat customer.

That paragraph sums up the major component visions of Best Image Printing and provides a good description of what the owner wants his company to be in 12 months or so. As you read through this book, you will follow the work that Best Image does as the owner and staff strive to attain this vision.

It is important to keep in mind that the individual component visions and the overall vision are based on your very best thinking, projections and available data _at this time_. Probably many of the component parts will change over the coming months, and Phase V of The MNM Process will guide you through any revisioning work that is necessary.

With your company's overall and component visions in place, you can now begin Phase II, developing the preliminary strategies that you'll use to achieve these visions.

Developing the Preliminary Long-Term Strategy

CONCEPTS TO GUIDE THE DEVELOPMENT OF YOUR PRELIMINARY LONG-TERM STRATEGY

Perhaps the most challenging aspect of the staff meetings that comprise the next phase of The MNM Process is that they *promote major change* within your business, both for you and for your staff. Your role in these staff meetings will be particularly challenging, as you must play a *dual* role. On one hand you are still the same shop owner, having the same daily responsibilities. On the other hand, you must assume a new role of *chief change agent*. This role will require you to facilitate, coach and nurture the growth and evolution of your staff, both as individuals and as a team.

When people perceive that change is in the making, they generally respond by erecting barriers, either consciously or unconsciously. In order for you to be effective in your new role, you must be totally comfortable with the major concepts of change that you will be working with, and have a clear personal understanding as to how these concepts fit in with your mission and overall management philosophy. In short, you must be willing to practice what you preach.

On the following pages we will look at the major concepts which will guide your work in the next phase of The MNM Process, and which are an important ingredient in the development of your preliminary long-term strategies for achieving your overall ideal vision.

Personal Management and Decision Making Styles

The MNM Process places great value in empowering individual employees to take on increasing responsibility and accountability for decision making in performing their work. The fundamental concept is that self-managing teams of empowered individuals can be extremely effective in increasing overall productivity and improving quality (and will also allow you the time you need to both market and manage your business). Before your

52

Figure 8.1 ■ **MANAGEMENT STYLE CHOICES**

	MANAGEMENT BY DECREE	MANAGEMENT BY SOLICITATION	MANAGEMENT BY PARTICIPATION	MANAGEMENT BY DELEGATION	MANAGEMENT BY DEFAULT
ROLE OF OWNER	Makes all policy Makes all strategy Makes all decisions	Asks for staff input Still makes major policy and strategy Still makes most decisions	Actively involves staff in making policy, strategy and decisions Joint effort process	Empowers staff to make more and more of their own decisions Acts as coach, facilitator and resource	Abandons leadership Leaves everything to staff
ROLE OF STAFF	Work hard and don't ask questions	Provides input on issues when asked	Work with owner in making some policy, strategy and decisions	Take on increasing responsibility for running business	Carry on as best they can Eventually blamed for failure of business
ROLE OF TEAMS	TEAMWORK IMPOSSIBLE	TEAMWORK POSSIBLE	SELF-MANAGING TEAMS POSSIBLE		INDIVIDUAL COMPETITION
RESULTS EXPECTED	Variable Limited effectiveness Depends on company culture	INCREASED PRODUCTIVITY IMPROVED QUALITY INCREASED INNOVATION AND CREATIVITY INCREASED STAFF ACCOUNTABILITY AND RESPONSIBILITY INCREASED STAFF PRIDE IN WORKMANSHIP			Probable failure of business

staff can become self managing and able to make their own decisions, you, as owner, will face your greatest challenge of The MNM Process: *accepting the risk that comes with letting go or giving up control.*

In this section you need to come to grips with this idea and develop some guidelines as to *how much* you are willing to let go in terms of your authority and managerial decision making.

A friend once told me about his first *real* job in high school, that of stock clerk in a small, neighborhood grocery store. He was really proud of this new job and eagerly tried to learn as much as he could about the business. One day he was in the back room preparing crates of lettuce which were to be put on sale for 15 cents a head. Being a sixteen-year-old, my friend didn't understand how the owner could sell the lettuce so cheaply, so when the store owner happened by, my friend asked him. The shop owner, a gruff, intimidating sort of man, answered something like, "Hey, let's get something straight right now: *I'm* the boss and *I* make the decisions; you're the employee and you do the work, ya got it? So, get on with it!" The employee got it alright, well enough that it was only a couple of weeks later that he managed to get something else: a new job at a competing grocery store down the street. A strong, forceful management style? You bet! An effective management style which encourages loyal employees who take pride and interest in their work? Not likely! Perhaps a case can be made for *management by decree* yielding results, but there never was a time when it yielded excellence.

The management style described above is one extreme in how decisions are made in business. The other extreme would be the various forms of absentee management where the owner routinely abandons all leadership roles and goes off to play golf or whatever, leaving all the decision making to the staff, *whether or not they have the training or experience to make decisions.* Probably all of us could cite several businesses which have tried to operate using this *management by default* practice. Probably none of us could cite a case where it has proven successful!

Management by Decree and *Management by Default* are two ways of managing a business. Between these two extremes are several other choices in personal management and decision making styles. As shown in figure 8.1, these choices are: *Management by Solicitation, Management by Participation,* and *Management by Delegation.* As the figure explains, these management styles are based on the increasing degree to which you choose to involve your staff in strategy and decision making.

In Management by Decree the shop owner retains all authority. In the Solicitation, Participation and Delegation styles progressively more authority is given to the staff until the owner's role has evolved into that of coach, facilitator and resource. In the extreme Management by Default style, the owner has abandoned all leadership and authority, leaving the staff to struggle with decisions that they probably are not capable of handling, so that ultimately the business flounders and even fails.

As you look at the management style choices shown in figure 8.1, where can you put yourself right now? You may want to make a note of it, and then refer to the management style chart a few months from now to see if you have changed. At some point, you may even ask your staff to tell you how they perceive your style!

Where you place your present management style is not as important as *how committed* you are to exploring the potential benefit to your business of staff participation and self-managing teams. Obviously, to explore the process at all will require you to give up *some* of your authority. However, this relinquishing or *sharing* of your power and authority will be explored gradually, so at no time should you feel greatly threatened.

In Chapter 9 you will develop a preliminary long-term strategy for achieving each of the eight component visions you developed in Chapter 7. Then you will determine which parts of those strategies you can comfortably share with your staff and which parts will not be shared.

Before going on to that work, let's take a closer look at the concept of self-managing teams.

Self-Managing Teams

Self-managing teams are groups of people who have a good understanding of the route that a job takes through the business from start to finish (the process path). They can work together *without supervision* to get the job done. They know what their teammates' roles are and commonly have some degree of cross-training, so that they can pitch in and help one another when required.

Self-managing teams do not have to be teams of people all doing the same thing. In fact, in most small businesses, such as a printshop, the team would consist of people having very different functions—press operator, customer service rep, bindery person, typesetter, etc. The distinguishing criteria of these teams, however, is that each individual considers the final product as being a result of their *combined team efforts*. To achieve this team-effort product, self-managing teams routinely engage in joint problem solving and make numerous decisions on their own without requiring or seeking constant advice from management.

Businesses best suited for self-managing teams are those which produce a product or service involving several sequential, complicated steps performed by different people. (This makes printshops ideal candidates). Self-managing teams are only effective if the team perceives that management (in this case you, the owner) is truly committed to the concept. This means that you must not only encourage your staff to solve more of their own problems and make their own decisions, but—and this is the difficult part—you must be willing to allow the team members to make, *without blame or punishment*, the numerous mistakes that will inevitably develop. When mistakes are made, you must be willing to patiently explore, discuss and explain what went wrong in a way that the team thoroughly understands, so that (hopefully) the mistake will not happen again. Initially this role of coach and teacher will demand much of your time. As the team begins to shift more and more into a self-managing mode, however, you will find you have more time available to manage your business.

A simple and helpful concept you can use in nurturing self-managing teams is *internal customers*. Each successive person in the production sequence is considered to be the internal customer of the previous person who has worked on the product. For example, the typesetter is the internal customer of the counter person; the press operator is, in turn, the internal customer of the typesetter, and so on.

The concept that you are building, and one which your staff will readily understand, is that as an internal customer they have the right to expect the same kind of quality and service that the external customer (the person who walks in the door) receives. Once your staff has accepted this concept, it is surprising what it alone can do for improving quality. When the internal customer concept is combined with a fully functioning self-managing team, the results can be truly impressive.

As is shown in figure 8.1, self-managing teams become possible when the management style is one that involves a high degree of *solicitation* of staff input. These teams become increasingly more effective as the management style moves into the *participation* and *delegation* modes. Phase III of The MNM Process is designed so that the shift to a self-managing team is made in a natural way, without fanfare. While you will probably want to discuss the internal customer concept, it's not necessary to even use the term self-managing team unless you so desire. Instead you will find that by the end of Phase III, your staff will have quietly evolved on its own into a self-managing team.

Again, it should be pointed out that the *degree* to which you take the self-managing aspect is left totally up to you. In this you have and always will have, total control.

A final resulting benefit of self-managing teams is increased *innovation* and *creativity*. Once the team begins functioning, you may notice that your staff is beginning to come up with more innovative and creative ideas for accomplishing their work. Innovation and creativity are a precious asset for any business and should be carefully nurtured. Your challenge here will be how to best utilize and develop this innovation in a way that is rewarding for both the business and the contributing individual. We will look into this in Phase IV.

Total Quality Systems: *The* Business Standard for the 1990s

American business has at last discovered—or re-discovered—quality. No matter where you look, the words Total Quality are the substance of today's American advertising message. And it's not likely to change. Big business has finally come to understand, after years of pompous denial, that Americans desire and will support *and pay for* quality.

What is Total Quality? Quite simply it means that quality becomes the standard for all planning, decision making and action throughout the company, for every person at every level. Strategically, it means placing the customer's (both external and internal) wants, needs and concerns first by providing maximum value and satisfaction in product and service at all times. To achieve Total Quality in this sense is definitely a major undertaking. Will it be worth it? The numerous companies around the country who have already made the effort say that it is.

Japan offers an international quality competition award, the Deming Prize, named for W. Edwards Deming, an American engineering professor who carried his quality concepts to Japan immediately following World War II after being totally ignored in this country. The Japanese, their economy literally in ashes, eagerly embraced Deming's concepts, and the rest is history. Now American business is rushing to catch up. In 1989 Florida Power and Light Company became the first non-Japanese company to win the Deming Prize.

Recognizing the positive effects of the Deming Prize competition, in 1987 Congress passed a bill establishing the Malcolm Baldridge Award as the U. S. equivalent to spur interest in quality in this country. Like the Deming Prize, the Malcolm Baldridge Award is recognized by its winners as offering a significant competitive advantage. Currently, Federal Express (the first award winner in the service sector) and Cadillac are using the award as a regular part of their advertising campaigns. No question about it, big business sees *big value* in Total Quality.

So, if quality is to be the new standard for American business, what can or should the smaller business owner like you do to move your business in the direction of Total Quality? What kind of method should be used, and how far do you need to carry it?

Good questions, these, and ones which you and your staff will explore in Phases III and IV of The MNM Process. Ultimately, you might choose to adopt or modify Deming's concepts, or keep it very simple like the *Golden Rule* or the *When In Doubt, Do What's Right* approach. Most likely, however, you—like your self-managing team—will find that the guiding principles for your shop's quality statement will evolve rather effortlessly as a by-product of participating in The MNM Process. The reason that this could be possible is quite simple. As the man said, "we all know what is the right thing to do, we just don't do it."

Other Concepts

Management styles, self-managing teams, internal customers and total quality are some of the major concepts and ideas which you and your staff will be considering during the Phase III and IV work. The other major concept of alignment of short-term action plans and long-term strategies will be taken up in Chapter 14. There are several other important concepts, such as a win/win customer service and the benefits of nurturing greater customer and vendor loyalty and support, which we'll take up as we go along.

Now let's turn to developing your preliminary long-term strategy for achieving the component visions of your business which you created in the last chapter.

DEVELOPING YOUR PRELIMINARY LONG-TERM STRATEGY

A number of years ago there was a funny cartoon making the rounds of construction and engineering companies. This cartoon depicted two surveyors thrashing around, waist-deep in water, in the middle of a jungle, with threatening snakes and alligators on every side. The caption read, "When you're up to your neck in alligators, it's hard to remember that your original objective was to drain the swamp!"

Probably quite a lot of people in other businesses can relate to that cartoon as well. Unfortunately, it epitomizes a dilemma which many companies face: habitual, panic-based, short-term actions which are in no way related to long-term goals. For many businesses, *fighting alligators* seems to be a never-ending way of life, regardless of what wonderful long-term strategy might be lying around in the company's filing cabinet. Yet, short-term and long-term strategies don't have to be at odds with one another.

In this chapter you will develop *preliminary* long-term strategies for achieving each of the component visions you developed in Chapter 7, using those vision statements as the basis for the strategies. Your overall preliminary long-term strategy will evolve from these individual strategies.

The individual strategies you develop here will be very specific about the actions you want to take over the next 12 to 18 months and will integrate into the work you'll do in Phase III of The MNM Process. These preliminary strategies will ensure that the short-term action plans and solutions which you will also develop in Phase III are in alignment with the overall long-term strategies that ultimately evolve.

Developing a Preliminary Strategy for Your Products and Services

Using your vision worksheet and vision statement for products and services (Chapter 7), you can now draw up a preliminary long-term strategy

Figure 9.1 ■ **STRATEGY FOR ACHIEVING VISION FOR PRODUCTS & SERVICES** / Best Image Printing

PROPOSED GOAL	PROPOSED OBJECTIVE	REQUIRED ACTION	REQUIRED CAPITAL	SOURCE OF CAPITAL	STARTING DATE	COMPLETION DATE
EXPAND EXISTING PRINTING CAPABILITY	Buy new press	Research and purchase press	$25,000 to $30,000	Commercial loan from bank	Begin talking to bank 6/1	Order press as soon as financing is arranged
	Install new press	Make room by moving platemaker into converted storage room	None		8/1	8/5
	Convert storage room	Redesign space to accommodate platemaker and contact builder	$1,500	Cash flow	7/15	7/30
	Hire press operator	Contact area technical schools	None		7/1	start work 7/15
EXPAND HIGH SPEED COPYING CAPABILITY	Install additional high speed copier	Research and choose equipment	?	Lease or rent from vendor	Immediate—3/18	Install ASAP
DEVELOP COLOR COPYING CAPABILITY	Install color copier	Research and choose equipment	$10,000 to $20,000	Lease/purchase thru vendor	Begin research 9/1	Install 12/1
ADD COLOR GRAPHICS CAPABILITY	Install color computer	Research equipment	?	Loan or lease	Begin research 10/1	2/1
EXPAND BINDERY CAPABILITY	Purchase new cutter	Research new and used equipment	?	?	Begin research 5/1	12/1

for achieving your ideal vision. Let Best Image Printing's strategy serve as a guide and notice how they first defined a goal,* then an objective, and then carried them out as far as necessary, with the end result being an action plan.

As you develop this strategy for products and services, keep in mind that it is *preliminary*. If you have difficulty with some parts, or are uncertain about possible alternatives, simply put down what seems reasonable for now. In Phase III you will be doing work which will add considerable clarity to any parts of the strategy which may be sketchy right now. It is important, however, that you take enough time on this exercise to make the outline of your strategy for your products and services *comprehensive*. It is far better to have a general strategy covering all of your products and services rather than a detailed strategy that focuses on only one or two products.

Once you have completed your preliminary strategy, you should type it and save it for future use. Before you put it in your binder, there is one more step you should complete for this and for the other preliminary strategies that you develop in this exercise. Make a copy of your strategy and using three color marking pens go back over your strategy, circling each element with the appropriate color as you ask yourself the following questions:

1) which of the elements of the strategies listed am I willing to *share fully* in discussions with my staff as part of the Phase III work,

2) which of the elements am I willing to *share in part*, and

3) which of the elements am I *not willing to share* at all with my staff at this time.

For example, consider goal 1 in figure 9.1, expanding existing printing capability. As owner you might feel totally comfortable in sharing the fact that the shop would be getting a new press and when it might be expected, but, perhaps, you might not be willing to discuss the actual cost of this equipment other than saying that it's quite expensive. Likewise, you may feel the source of capital you use to purchase the press is privileged information.

When you begin facilitating the work of Phase III, it will help you immeasurably if you have considered the sensitivity of each of these strategic elements in advance, before the issues arise in the staff meetings. In building a self-managing team, it is critical to have consistent, well-understood ground rules on what is and is not an area of concern or responsibility for your staff.

---

* As used in this book, a *goal* constitutes the desired *overall end* to which your effort is directed and which may or may not be achieved as envisioned. An *objective*, by contrast, is a *specific aspect or task* which has a high probability of being achieved.

Figure 9.2 ■ **STRATEGY FOR ACHIEVING VISION FOR IDEAL CUSTOMER BASE** / Best Image Printing

PROPOSED GOAL	PROPOSED OBJECTIVE	REQUIRED ACTION	START DATE	FINISH DATE
EXPAND CUSTOMER BASE BY 20%—focus particularly on recession-proof customers	*Identify recession-proof businesses and customer groups and prepare target list of 5 best potential customer groups that also are in alignment with company mission and meet ideal customer criteria.*	*Contact Small Business Administration, state Economic Development Office, local Chamber of Commerce for historical information. Compare data with company and other print industry experience to determine potential for meeting ideal customer criteria ranking.*	*4/1*	*4/15*
	Develop marketing plan.	*Develop targeted sales and advertising materials for each of the 5 customer groups. (Consider hiring a professional advertising specialist.)*	*4/19*	*5/1*
	Implement marketing plan.	*Begin personal sales calls where appropriate. Begin targeted mailings. Join area civic and business organizations.*	*5/2*	*6/15*
INCREASE PERCENTAGE OF REPEAT CUSTOMERS	*Poll former customers to find out reasons for lost business.*	*Develop questionnaire which can be done by mail or in phone interviews and begin using it.*	*4/15*	*5/7*
	Synthesize results from poll and develop plan of corrective action.	*Utilize Phase III of The MNM Team Building Process to solicit input for corrective action.*	*5/21*	*6/21*

A second reason for deciding what to share is that in considering the sensitivity of each of your proposed strategies, you will develop a more objective understanding of *your* personal management style. In this way you can open up an internal dialog as to *why* you perceive the issues the way you do, and whether or not there might be any merit for a change in your attitude.

Developing a Preliminary Strategy for Achieving Your Ideal Customer Base

Using the same procedure as above, you should now develop a preliminary long-term strategy for your ideal customer base. Again, let Best Image Printing's strategy (figure 9.2) serve as a guide.

Once you have developed a strategy for achieving your ideal customer base, you should again carefully review your final product to determine which elements you are willing to share with your staff in the up-coming meetings. Many business owners tend to be very secretive about their customer base. Some clients have told me that they never let *anyone* know details about their customers, including their employees. While this concern is understandable, the suggestion that is offered here is that the more your employees are involved with the details of a customer, the more attentive they are in meeting their needs. Again, a primary objective of The MNM Process is to develop customers who are so loyal to your business that they tell *everyone* what a super printer you are!

Developing a Preliminary Strategy for Your Physical Facilities

Using the 12-month vision for physical facilities that you developed in Chapter 7, and perhaps some of your work from the previous exercises, you should now write down the strategic steps necessary to attain that vision. Figure 9.3 presents Best Image Printing's strategy for their physical facilities.

Developing a Preliminary Strategy for Your Equipment

Much of the work that you've done so far in this chapter should be applicable to developing a strategy for the equipment component of the overall vision for your business. In developing your preliminary equipment strategy you might find that a combination of the formats presented in figures 9.1 and 9.2 would be useful.

Figure 9.3 ■ **STRATEGY FOR ACHIEVING VISION FOR PHYSICAL FACILITIES** / Best Image Printing

PROPOSED GOAL	PROPOSED OBJECTIVE	REQUIRED ACTION	START DATE	FINISH DATE
EXPAND SHOP SPACE BY 150 SQ. FT. FOR NEW PRESS	Convert storage room to accommodate platemaker; put press where platemaker is now	Redesign space Contact contractor Begin remodelling	6/1 6/15 7/15	 7/30
EXPAND SPACE BY 100 SQ. FT. FOR NEW HIGH SPEED COPIER	Redesign front customer space and work space to accommodate equipment	Rearrange furniture and equipment	4/1	4/21
BETTER APPEARANCE	New carpet, paint, etc.	Assemble estimates and do work	4/1	12/1
MORE VISIBILITY	New sign	Get estimates	4/1	6/1

In addition to new equipment, you would also want to consider existing equipment in your strategy. The old saying, "but for the want of a nail, the battle was lost" is most appropriate in this aspect of your strategic planning. It's very frustrating for any business owner to watch a customer walk out the door with an order you had to turn down because the needed equipment was waiting for a 75¢ part. It's important to keep your equipment in top shape; a preventive maintenance plan coupled with an inventory of critical spare parts and supplies, plus *effective* service contracts on major equipment, can account for a significant decrease in down time. In addition, the credibility you build with your customers by doing their work when they need it one of the best forms of advertising you can have.

In developing your strategy for equipment be sure to devote sufficient time to brainstorming for new and innovative approaches to old problems. Perhaps Best Image's strategies will help get you started.

Best Image Printing
Preliminary Strategy for Equipment

— *Research and add new equipment as planned.*

— *Implement an equipment failure monitoring system to get an objective picture of which equipment, parts and systems are causing repetitive downtime.*

— *Ask each staff member to develop a preventive maintenance system for their equipment using equipment manuals and conversations with the equipment manufacturer.*

— *Send the staff to trade shows with the task of thoroughly investigating equipment in their area of expertise and developing appropriate product literature files.*

— *Investigate setting up reciprocal emergency use plans with other printing shops or complementary businesses— computer, photographic, textbook binders, etc. [Many large service companies and non-profits have in-house capabilities. Also, today's expanded overnight delivery services permit reciprocal work outside of your competitive area, which was never before possible.]*

— *Explore possibilities for the shop being designated a regional test facility for new equipment just entering the market.*

Developing a Preliminary Strategy for Your Staff

The vision for staff that you developed in Chapter 7 will be greatly modified as you become involved in the Phase III work. In a sense, *all* of Phase III could be considered the preliminary strategy for your ideal staff vision for the time being. Nevertheless, there is still strategic preparatory work that can be done now by taking the time to consider each element you noted in your staff vision and come up with appropriate strategies. The work you did in developing your strategy for products and services considered the question of additional staff that might be needed to provide your envisioned products and services, but your strategy for attaining your staff vision should also include existing staff.

Best Image Printing
Preliminary Strategy for Staff

- *Implement The MNM Team Building Process and read other available material on self-managing teams.*

- *Maintain an active file of possible candidates for all positions.* [In a small shop the sudden loss of one person can cause major disruption.]

- *Get to know the instructors at local trade and art schools. Make sure they know all about my shop and the high quality work we do so they can bring superior graduates to my attention.*

- *Make sure our help wanted ads are in alignment with both the shop's mission and the ideal vision for the particular staff person needed.* [It's far better to spend more time in selective hiring than to try to change a person over to your style of business management.]

- *Investigate training programs offered by local schools, equipment manufacturers and private companies to ensure that our staff has the best in state-of-the-art skills and education.*

- *Read available books about the various new types of incentive systems that are being implemented around the country.*

- *Add staff to accommodate growth.*

Developing a Preliminary Strategy for Your Vendors

In this exercise you will develop an initial strategy for attaining your vision of the ideal vendor component of your business which you created in Chapter 7. Certainly not all vendors use the principles of business that we are discussing in this book. Many, obviously, do not yet see the strategic advantage of "total quality customer service," and are firmly entrenched in playing a win/lose game (when I win, you lose)—and you know who is the loser. However, just like your staff, *some* of these vendors can be coached, encouraged and taught to see the mutual value in putting your needs ahead of their own personal agenda. Does it take a lot of time and effort to change them? Yes. Is it worth it? Sometimes. Depends on your alternatives and your personal nature. As Joe Collier, former CEO of Florida Power & Light, is fond of quoting regarding the major changes his company went through in pursuing the concept of total quality, "Sometimes we found it easier to change people than to change people." So it depends on your options. Unfortunately, when it comes to certain suppliers, smaller printers generally don't have much to choose from or change to. When that's the case, you have everything to gain and nothing to lose by trying to encourage a vendor to do the right thing.

Best Image Printing
Preliminary Strategy for Vendors

- *Initiate a systematic search and evaluation of all existing and potential vendors within our area from whom we have not previously purchased products.*

- *Develop and implement a plan to gradually demonstrate the value of playing a win/win game [when I win, you also win] to my most problematic vendors.*

- *Contact our closest non-competitive shops and organizations with in-house printing facilities to explore the potential of combining orders to get better price breaks.*

- *Institute a Vendor of the Month Award in our shop, complete with wall plaque, certificate of appreciation for the company representative and letters to the vendor's president.*

Developing a Preliminary Strategy for Marketing and Sales

The preliminary strategy that you develop for marketing and sales will, of course, be closely tied to the strategy that you developed for achieving your ideal customer base. Developing an effective marketing strategy is an intensely challenging undertaking for any business. One of your best strategies—and your least costly—is enthusiastic, boastful customers who constantly refer new customers to you, and who would never think of giving their business to anyone else. Basically, the heart of the matter is *quality speaks louder than words*. The MNM Process is focused on building this kind of credibility and reputation for your business. Total customer service when coupled with the goal of *never lose a customer* makes an unbeatable marketing and sales strategy.

In Phases III and IV you will have ample opportunity to explore how to implement the above strategies in your business. However, for now you are asked to give some thought to creating your initial strategies for the marketing and sales vision that you developed.

Best Image Printing
Preliminary Strategy for Marketing and Sales

- *Implement a customer satisfaction monitoring scheme which provides reliable feedback on a regular basis to help eliminate losing customers.*

- *Focus 50% of our marketing effort on five new customer group segments as identified by my marketing research.*

- *Interview marketing and advertising agencies in town to ascertain capabilities and individual specialties relative to developing effective new marketing materials for the targeted customer groups which we have identified. Look into the possibility of trading services.*

- *Attend meetings and trade shows of targeted customer groups to better understand their wants and needs.*

- *Develop a special promotion, (i.e., 3¢ high speed copies or free color ink) for each of the four targeted customer groups and saturate the market by direct mail.*

- *Focus a large portion of our charity and community service work during the coming year on new projects which are effective in reaching the attention of the targeted customer groups.*

Developing a Preliminary Strategy for Your Competition

In this final exercise you are asked to write down your preliminary strategy for achieving your ideal vision regarding competition. As stated earlier, The MNM Process does not focus intensely on what the competition is doing. Instead the emphasis is on *listening to your customers*. They can and will, if given the chance, tell you many things you need to know. You can then supplement this information with your own research on your competition.

Best Image Printing
Preliminary Strategy for Competition

- *Define the existing market niche of competition relative to ours.*

- *Develop pricing/quality/service matrix analysis for competitions' products and services relative to ours.*

- *Ask our repeat customers what they like best about our services (why they continue to use us).*

> *– Hire independent survey consultant to poll businesses in town and do a marketing survey to determine customers' attitudes, preferences and complaints about existing local printing services.*

Developing a Preliminary Overall Long-Term Strategy for Attaining Your Company's Vision

Once you have finished creating each of the component strategies for your business, you need to synthesize them into a preliminary overall long-term strategy. This overall strategy should capture the essence of each of the component strategies, but will not include every detail.

The process of abstracting your overall preliminary long-term strategy statement will also give you the chance to examine your individual component strategies for inconsistencies or conflicts between goals and objectives. If you find some, and you probably will, now is the time to think the problem through and correct it.

> **BEST IMAGE PRINTING'S**
> **PRELIMINARY LONG-TERM STRATEGY**
>
> *The preliminary, overall long-term strategy for Best Image Printing is to nurture our unique market niche by expanding our existing capabilities, particularly in color printing and high-speed copying; by retaining, expanding and recession-proofing our customer base; by building a self-managing team; and by developing reliable and dependable vendors.*

Summary

Once you have completed all of the exercises through Chapter 9, you have completed Phases I and II of The MNM Process. Before going on to Phase III, it might be worthwhile to take a look at where you are and how far you have come.

The work up until now has had two objectives. The first has been to develop clarity and an in-depth understanding for you as owner around the concepts of mission, vision and strategy—the whys, whats and hows of a business. The second objective has been to introduce some of the major concepts and theory behind The MNM Team Building Process in a practical way, which allowed you to think about them and work with them in developing some preliminary visioning and strategic planning. Basically, the goal of this work has been to develop a foundation, guidelines, and baseline which can be used to support and direct the work that you will be taking on in Phase III and IV.

In our discussion of management styles, we made a point of stressing that in the upcoming work there are no fixed boundaries or absolutes regarding degrees of shared responsibility and decision making that must be achieved for the process to work. Rather, the important thing is that as owner you are comfortable with the results of each stage of the process as it takes place and are willing to give the concepts of employee involvement and self-managing teams a chance to work. It *will* take time, and it *is* better if the work goes slowly rather than quickly.

If you look again at figure 2.1 (in Chapter 2), you will see a dashed line representing the Path of Progress towards the Ideal Vision. Up until now the path has simply followed the Productivity/Quality Baseline, your traditional and historical performance standard. Because you have been the only one involved in this preparatory work, nothing has been done to impact the work system. As Phase III begins, however, the system *will* be impacted and you can expect the Path of Progress to begin to move. It would be misleading to suggest that the Path of Progress will show a daily and steady climb towards increased productivity and improved quality. It would be nice, but it won't. There will be periods of time when the path will take a sharp turn *downward*. Quite possibly, particularly in the beginning, the path may drop *below* the productivity and quality baseline! If it does, you shouldn't be alarmed. This is to be expected, and the downturn should be only temporary. Again, the reason for fluctuations is that any time change is introduced into a system of people you can expect initial periods of uncertainty and confusion. Fortunately, however, there are ways for you to anticipate and minimize these downturns and they'll be discussed in detail in the next chapter, as work begins on Phase III.

BUILDING

THE

TEAM

PREPARING FOR YOUR STAFF MEETINGS

Now you are ready to begin the work which will ultimately increase production and improve quality within your printing business: the meetings between you and your staff. These meetings are the heart of Phase III of The MNM Process. In all likelihood, you will find your role in this work distinctly different from your role of owner.

At first you may find it a challenge to facilitate without judgement and coach without control. This is natural, and you shouldn't be too concerned. It will become easier after a few meetings. Possible pitfalls and problems and how to deal with them will be discussed as we work through each successive step of this phase. For now, it would be helpful to recognize that to the extent that *you* feel uncomfortable in your new role of facilitator and coach, your staff is probably experiencing the same degree of uncertainty and self-consciousness, and possibly more.

The Phase III implementation work has been broken down into two tasks:

Task 1:   Eight sessions focused on establishing an accurate and comprehensive profile of your business as it exists right now.

Task 2:   Six sessions focused on developing an ideal self-managing team.

Before you can begin working on Task 1, there is some preparatory work to do. You will need to determine where, when, for how long, and how often to meet. It will be very important for you to begin to build awareness within your staff around the work to be done. Once these issues have been thought out, you can get on to the meetings themselves.

Where to Hold the Meetings

One of the first issues you must deal with is *where* to have your meetings.

Few would argue that the location and physical environment chosen for a meeting can have a very pronounced outcome on the meeting. This is particularly true for meetings such as you will be conducting which involve a high degree of participatory involvement of all the people present.

The first decision is whether you should have the meetings at your shop or at an off-site location. There are many good reasons for having the meetings at your shop: minimal cost, minimal time requirements, ability to refer to equipment and facilities, and privacy. Disadvantages would include the difficulty for people to shift away from their normal work mode (and traditional interpersonal relationships), a formal environment which may not be conducive to good dialogue, lack of comfortable and adequate space, and possible work-related interruptions. Selection of the best location will require some thought on your part. One good way of approaching it, after you have thought about the options, is to raise the issue to your staff at your initial meeting. This would be a good way of demonstrating to them that they will definitely be having a say in the meeting process to come!

The point to remember is that there is *no right place* to hold the meetings. As will be pointed out again and again in this work, what is right is what works for you and for your group. Experience shows that both on-site and off-site meetings can work equally well. One idea is to have your first meeting at an off-site place, which lets the group know that they really are setting off together on a new, exciting and *different* journey. Then, unless there are serious objections, have the meetings at the shop and save the off-site locations to emphasize or celebrate reaching the end of certain tasks or milestones in the process. You can always move off-site if you see that, for whatever reason, meeting in your shop is not working.

When, How Long, and How Often to Meet

There are no hard and fast rules to use in deciding when, how long, and how often to meet. Experience has shown that two-hour meetings are about the right length of time—any shorter is not productive, any longer and people get antsy.

The when part is certainly your and your staff's call. In most cases a two-hour block of time immediately following the day's work is best for most people. It is most important that everyone be present for every meeting, so there will have to be some flexibility in order to accommodate changes in individual schedules. If you choose Monday evenings for your meetings, everyone must be prepared to occasionally switch to some other evening when conflicts interfere. It is important that the meetings are undertaken with a certain amount of formality and that the staff consider this work a serious part of their job responsibility.

With respect to how often, the suggestion would be every two weeks for the duration of Phase III and every three weeks for Phase IV. Again, it is possible to meet more often, but no more than once a week. Longer intervals are not advisable because the process becomes disjointed, loses continuity, and people lose interest.

Meeting Style

It is desirable for the meetings to have some degree of formal structure, but it is even more important that they take place in a relaxed, highly spontaneous, and above all, enjoyable atmosphere. Thus the style in which the meetings are conducted becomes a significant issue. As facilitator, you have a challenging role in making sure that the meetings are productive by conducting them in a way that every member of your staff wants to and is encouraged to have input. Remember: it is you as facilitator who sets the tone of the meetings.

Here are some suggestions which you might consider as guidelines concerning the style of The MNM meetings.

- **Provide food and refreshments:** Depending on where and when your meetings are held, you will want to give some serious thought to food and refreshments. The nature of the MNM meetings is such that the provision of good refreshments can be very helpful in maintaining enthusiasm and active participation. It will not interfere with the work, and can actually serve to break down some of the barriers between people and promote greater input. People may be tired after working all day, but knowing that there will be something good to eat can make a big difference in attitude. It doesn't have to be a banquet—pizzas and soft-drinks delivered to a meeting at the shop can be a great way of easing the transition from work mode to meeting mode.

- **Encourage staff input:** As owner, your knowledge and understanding of most issues *is* better than that of your staff. In most cases, this is understood and doesn't have to be constantly demonstrated. Instead, try to encourage your staff to explain how and why *they* feel and think the way they do about an issue, even though you may think that their understanding is naive or limited. As much as possible, save *your* thoughts and understanding for the *end* of these discussions, allowing each staff member time to state his views. Remember that for some of your staff, being asked for thoughts and ideas may be a new experience, and it is quite natural for this input to evolve slowly and hesitatingly until confidence builds. If, after discussing an issue for a while, you feel that the group is getting off base, *then* bring in your knowledge and understanding. This should be done in a way that does not degrade or belittle the contributions your staff has made on the subject but instead adds to or offers additional understanding on their perspectives. In other words, give your staff the knowledge, or at least an appreciation, of the experience that leads you to think and feel the way you do, and do it in a way that maintains *value* for their contribution. Again, *you are not giving up your power* as owner by doing this. Instead, you are *utilizing it in a new way* to empower and nurture your staff to think, act and create more responsibly on their own.

— **Keep the dialogue going but encourage spontaneity:** When you are facilitating the meetings, let people continue to talk as long as the discussion is relevant and productive. It is important to follow an agenda, but cutting off conversation for the sake of moving on defeats the purpose of the meetings. Remember, you are building a team, not getting an order out the door!

— **Stay relaxed and enjoy yourself:** Again, as facilitator you set the tone of the meetings. If you are tense and impatient, it will show and the whole meeting can become a rather mechanical exercise yielding only the predictable. By staying relaxed and approaching the meetings with a certain amount of playfulness, you will be amazed at the synergy and creativity that develops.

Compensation

Another issue concerns the matter of pay for attending the meetings. Because there is no practical way of conducting The MNM Process during regular working hours, this means that you will be paying overtime wages for the two-hour sessions. Now this may seem like a significant cost, but it really isn't.

Basically, you are looking at paying approximately 40 hours of overtime per staff member for a year's participation in the process (14 sessions or 28 hours for Phase III and 6 sessions or 12 hours for Phase IV). Using an average hourly rate of $9.00 ($13.50 overtime), this comes to $540.00 per staff member. Adding an additional $110 per person for pizza and soft drinks would bring the total cost to $650 per person for a year, or about $4,000 for a staff of six.

This isn't much when you consider that The MNM Process should increase productivity by at least 10% in the first year. (If your sales are $350,000, that's a $35,000 increase.) How that increase in sales affects your bottom line is ultimately up to you, but if you become capable of producing more work faster, you should see more profits.

Developing Initial Staff Awareness and Commitment in The MNM Process

We recommend you read this entire book before beginning to implement The MNM Process with your staff. Once you have a good personal understanding of the process, you can begin to build interest and commitment among your staff for getting involved in the process themselves.

Once you have decided to go ahead with the process, you need to tell your staff. There are a number of ways you can do this:

1. You could simply tell your staff that the business is going to involve itself in a new training program and the first meeting will be next Monday after work.

2. You could take several weeks to informally and indirectly introduce some of the concepts on which The MNM Process is based. You might hand out reprints of some articles which talk about the great successes other companies have been having in utilizing concepts such as total quality, win/win customer service, and self-managing teams.

3. You could send or take some of your staff to a one-day seminar, talk or workshop on one or several of the concepts that are involved in The MNM Process. Many organizations (such as the Chamber of Commerce, your local chapter of the American Society for Quality Control, or business colleges and universities) frequently offer programs geared to the business community which can serve as catalysts for embarking on The MNM Process.

4. You could schedule the start of the meetings immediately following a meeting of your local printing trade association which you and your staff would attend together.

Whatever method you use, the general objective is to *begin building interest and awareness of some of the larger issues which all of your staff face in their profession, while at the same time informally introducing some of The MNM Process concepts to them in the shop.*

Planning How You Will Introduce The MNM Process

Once you think you have succeeded in arousing interest and curiosity about these ideas on an informal basis, then the next step would be to involve your staff in a meeting, perhaps at an off-site location, for the purpose of formally introducing them to some new *possibilities* which you have been exploring for the company based on the ideas you have been telling them about. At this meeting you can lay out the outline of The MNM Process—the benefits as well as the difficulties and requirements—and ask if there would be group interest in *participating* in such a process.

Prior to holding this meeting, it probably would be useful if you put together some handouts or overhead projector transparencies which give a clear picture and understanding of what the process is about and what benefits can be expected. Feel free to use any of the figures or information used in this book. Certainly this is a great time to unveil the new mission and vision statements that you worked so hard on!

Some of the materials you might want to prepare for this initial meeting would be:

- Phases of The MNM Process (figure 2.1, page 8)
- The Expected Results and Benefits of The MNM Process (page 5-6)
- Definitions of Mission, Vision and Strategy (figure 3.1, page 18)
- Your Mission Statement (as developed in Chapter 6)
- Your Overall Vision for Your Business (as developed in Chapter 7)

If you have done your homework and laid the groundwork well, this initial meeting will go very smoothly and you'll have no difficulty in obtaining the necessary commitment from your staff to go forward with The MNM Process. Ideally, you would conclude the meeting with the logistic issues settled and a meeting schedule worked out.

Suggested Format for Phase III Meetings

All of us have attended meetings where we spent the whole time wishing we were somewhere else, so it is important that each of the meetings in The MNM Process be approached with thoughtful planning and preparation. Here are a few ideas that will help make your facilitation of The MNM Process meetings more successful.

- **Develop a Phase III meeting schedule outline.** Before the first meeting, spend some time putting together a schedule and outline of topics for all of the Phase III meetings. Initially you might want to base your schedule and outline on the order of topics presented in this book, but do so with the understanding that you can modify this at any time once you get started.

- **Have a firm agenda for each meeting.** It is important that each meeting have an agenda so that your staff can be thinking about the topics to be covered. While conducting the meeting, make sure that the group stays focused on the agenda. As we said earlier, staff input and discussion is to be encouraged and not cut off prematurely; but as facilitator, one of your primary functions is to keep the group focused on the subject at hand. If you see that there is merit in pursing a tangent, then bring this to the attention of the group, and if they agree, change the agenda accordingly.

- **Take comprehensive notes during the meeting.** You should invest in a light-weight, collapsible, flip-chart easel and several paper pads, if you don't already have them. (You can get by using odds and ends scrounged from your shop, but the hassle is not worth it.) A flip-chart is recommended, rather than simply taking notes on a pad of paper, because an objective of every session will be to develop *group-based ideas*. As thoughts are generated, they need to be captured in a manner that enables everyone to see them and build on them. Taping the flip-chart pages on the wall as you finish them helps people refer back to earlier ideas and shows that progress is being made. The flip-chart pages are the source of the minutes you'll develop after each meeting.

- **Develop comprehensive, formal minutes for each meeting.** Immediately following each meeting, one of your important functions as facilitator is to put together a comprehensive and formal record of everything discussed during the meeting. The value of this record to the success of the process cannot be overstated. In many meetings there will be numerous times when the ideas and concepts expressed are highly innovative and creative, and reflect a high level of consensus or synergy (1+1=3) within the group. By taking special pains to capture this individual and group innovation, the resulting record serves as a valuable feed-back mechanism to propel the group forward into greater interaction and participation.

  Generally it is not necessary or, in most cases, not even desirable to tie a particular comment or idea to a specific individual in the group. Because you are building a group *team*—not evaluating individuals— it is the work of the group that is important, not the work of the individual. There are, of course, exceptions to this.

   – **Provide a binder for each staff member to keep their minutes.** Providing a binder in which each staff member can keep their minutes and other handouts will add value to the work being done, as well as provide an on-going record of the changes that are taking place. Your staff will refer to these records more and more as time goes on, because they will serve as a reference point for monitoring the work that has been done, as well as the work still to be accomplished.

How to Conduct the Meetings

Prior to the first meeting, give everyone an agenda similar to Best Image Printing's agenda (see page 85). Your personal agenda—the one you'll use to facilitate the meetings—should be slightly more detailed, like this:

Owner's Agenda

1. Facilitate staff exploration of strengths of topic
2. Facilitate staff exploration of weaknesses of topic
3. Facilitate staff brainstorming on potential opportunities offered by each weakness
4. Compare and discuss staff's perceptions of strengths, weaknesses and opportunities with my own perceptions
5. Review and critique the work just done

Start the meeting by introducing the topic and considering first its strengths. On your flip chart, write "Strengths" across the top, and then number and list each response as it is suggested by your staff. Remember that your primary role is that of facilitator and save your input for the end of the session or for whenever the discussion lags.

When the group has exhausted their ideas on strengths, tear off the sheet and tape it to the wall nearby. You can add to the strengths at any time.

On a new sheet, write "Weaknesses" and repeat the process. Tape this sheet to the wall, also, when done.

Next, the weaknesses will be examined one by one and the opportunities offered by each will be listed. (You should start a new sheet labeled "Opportunities.") Brainstorming works best here. As facilitator, make sure your staff understands that the purpose of brainstorming is to generate as many ideas as possible on a topic in a short period of time, without judgement. In brainstorming, even wild or crazy ideas are encouraged, as they can trigger innovative ideas that really work. After the brainstorming is done, as a group or by yourself, you can go over the ideas and separate out the more useful ones.

When it is apparent that the group has gone as far as they can in eliminating less promising opportunities, you should then reexamine each of the remaining opportunities and place them into the following three categories:

Immediate opportunities that can be implemented now.

Short-term opportunities that can be implemented over the next few weeks and months (Phase IV).

Long-term opportunities that will be implemented during the coming year (Phases IV and V).

Conclude this part of the work by focusing on the opportunities in the immediate category and determine who—shop owner, individual staff member, or team—will assume the responsibility for implementing them.

With the group work for the session completed, you can now introduce the vision statement you developed in Chapter 7. In all probability the work the group just finished will be similar or complementary to what you have done.

Your last responsibility as facilitator of MNM meetings is to see that each meeting has a proper ending. Accordingly, you should allow 10 minutes or so to review and evaluate what has been accomplished, observe how far you have proceeded on the agenda items, and discuss the agenda for the next meeting.

Part of this closing exercise should be to allow each staff member time for final input, particularly around the usefulness of the meeting and what could be done to improve it. Adjourn with a clear announcement as to when the next meeting will be and when the minutes from the meeting just finished will be ready.

Before You Start Each Meeting

Before each meeting you should review the appropriate vision and preliminary strategy that you prepared in Chapters 7 and 9. The question you need to ask yourself as you review these statements is what parts of this material you are willing to share with your staff. By considering this in advance for each topic, you will be able to concentrate more fully on your job as facilitator without feeling uncomfortable about possible discussions that might develop during the meetings.

It is recommended that you not share with your staff any of your vision or strategy work for any of the topics until *after* you have facilitated the staff's consideration of the strengths, weaknesses, and opportunities. This will eliminate any possible version of "The Queen's Mirror" effect from entering into the picture, as it is human nature for employees to tell the boss whatever it is that they think s/he wants to hear.

Your Role as Facilitator

Here are some things that you might want to keep in mind about facilitating meetings.

- Be a good *listener*, keep your input to a minimum
- Ask questions for *clarification*—don't assume you understand; again, mirrors can be deceptive
- Encourage *all* of your staff to participate, but don't push it
- Don't play favorites; a good facilitator is always *neutral*
- Don't be judgemental; at this stage, judgement is deadly!
- Be enthusiastic! Remember, *you* set the tone of the meeting
- Be relaxed and natural; a sure sign that the process is working is when it's obvious that people are *enjoying* the session
- Be sure to solicit feedback at the end of the meeting as to how the staff valued the meeting and what might be done to improve the next one
- End the meeting on time—leave them wanting more!

It is important that you get the minutes typed up in final form and back to your staff as quickly as possible after each meeting. This procedure will not only serve to increase interest in the process, but will once again emphasize your commitment. Where appropriate, include a well-defined action plan which breaks the discovered opportunities into the three categories of immediate, short-term and long-term action. If specific individuals are to be responsible for certain tasks or action, then be sure that this responsibility is clearly stated in the minutes.

CHAPTER 11

THE TASK 1 STAFF MEETINGS

At this point, all of your preparatory work is done. You've thought about and written down your mission, vision, and strategies; you've decided where, when, how often, and for how long you want to meet; and you've prepared everyone for what's to come. Now you're ready to begin the heart of The MNM Process: the bi-weekly meetings with your staff.

Your goal at these meetings is to allow your staff the freedom to express their thoughts and ideas. For the meetings that comprise Task 1, you have already written down your own thoughts and ideas in the form of your Phase II vision statements. Later you will compare your ideas to those of your staff and revise your component visions.

Each of the 14 sessions of Tasks 1 and 2 has been presented here as a single meeting. In reality, though, it is highly unlikely that each topic will take precisely two hours. With this in mind, it is desirable to prepare a single agenda for Task 1 and another for Task 2 that will encompass the entire task and allow you the freedom to give each topic whatever amount of time is necessary for it to be fully explored. Because you are keeping a detailed record of your meetings (the minutes), you can easily end a meeting in the middle of a topic and begin two weeks later right where you left off, with no loss of continuity. You can distribute this agenda at the beginning of each task, and save yourself the exercise of preparing individual meeting agendas.

Here is how you'll find each Task 1 and 2 staff meeting (or topic) presented:

1. Goals and Objectives
2. Preparatory Information, Learning or Action
3. Case Study Discussion and Analysis
4. Recommendations for Conducting the Meeting
5. Best Image Printing's Minutes

Remember: the purpose of these sessions is to encourage *your staff's* input and ideas, not yours.

Creating a "Snapshot In Time" of Your Business

Over 200 years ago Robert Burns said quite eloquently, "O wad some pow'r the giftie gie us/to see ourselves as others see us!" And, as the wicked queen in Snow White refused to acknowledge, many times the mirrors we choose to look in are not very reliable. Seeing ourselves exactly as we are is very, very difficult.

The overall goal of Task 1 is to obtain as accurate as possible a picture of the current state of your business. Unfortunately, for an owner the experience of trying to make an objective evaluation of the current status of his or her business can be just as difficult as the wicked queen trying to see herself. And if you think about it, how could it be otherwise? After all those countless hours of worry, struggle, and effort, is it exaggerating to suggest that as owner *you are too close to the business to really see it clearly*? Certainly not. For most small businesses, the identity of the owner and the business are one and the same.

Fortunately, for every owner there is a reliable mirror available in-house to use in obtaining an objective current status analysis of the business. That mirror is *your staff!* Granted, they don't have the same perspective as you do as owner. But that's just the point. *To the limits of their knowledge and understanding,* your staff sees quite clearly what is going on, precisely because they *don't* have your perspective. They are not as close to it as you are, so they don't identify with the business as you do. Their observations can have great value. Now the question becomes how do you obtain that input and what do you do with it once you get it. The answers to these questions are the essence of the work of the eight sessions of The MNM Process which comprise Task 1.

Using a "Snapshot In Time" approach, your staff will take a look at the company as it currently exists. They will look at the same components for which you developed your preliminary visions in Chapter 7. In order to overcome possible staff reticence and encourage greater participation, we will look at the components in a different order. This order will begin with the most familiar components, for which everyone will have input, and steadily progress to those requiring greater thought and contemplation. Your staff will not be asked to look at themselves in Task I, but will be the deferred focus of Task II.

Take a few minutes right now to look over Best Image Printing's background information. You should also review the agenda that the owner prepared for his staff prior to beginning their meetings. He used a concise, easy-to-follow format that outlined all of the Task 1 topics, but didn't go into the same detail as his personal agenda.

BEST IMAGE PRINTING

Best Image Printing is a four-year-old printing franchise located in a metropolitan city of about 100,000 people. At the time they began working on The MNM Process, the shop had a staff of six people, plus an owner/manager with over 15 years experience in the printing industry. Annual gross sales were $380,000. In spite of a recessionary economy, the shop was able to realize an increase in gross sales of 20% within six months of beginning The MNM Process.

In terms of management style, the owner of Best Image Printing is a firm believer in the Participation and Delegation modes (see figure 8.1), and places great value in sharing what he considers to be fundamental financial and economic data with his staff.

Here's the agenda that the owner prepared for his staff prior to the start of Session 1.

Best Image Staff Meetings
AGENDA

The purpose of these bi-weekly staff meetings is to conduct an in-house analysis of who we are and how we're doing.

To accomplish this, we will do an assessment consisting of an examination of our strengths and weaknesses, and then explore the opportunities offered by our weaknesses. You can think of this assessment as a snapshot of Best Image Printing circa 1989.

The major categories of the business which we will examine are:

- *facilities*
- *equipment*
- *products and services*
- *vendors*
- *customers*
- *competition*
- *marketing and sales*
- *general economic outlook*

Now that you know a little bit about Best Image Printing, let's take a look at Session 1.

Session 1
PHYSICAL FACILITIES

Goals and Objectives

Your goal in Session 1 is to develop an accurate appraisal of your current physical facilities by soliciting the combined observations and understanding of your staff and then integrating their appraisal into your own ideal vision for facilities.

The specific objective is to have your staff look at the strengths and weaknesses of your existing facilities, and then explore potential opportunities for growth or improvement offered by the weaknesses.

Preparatory Information, Learning or Action

Review your vision and preliminary strategy statements.

Case Study Discussion and Analysis

A significant issue for Best Image which emerged during this session, and one which would emerge in many of the sessions to come, was the issue of space. The company had grown considerably during the previous two years and had no room left for expansion. In terms of need, there was no question that additional space would be highly beneficial. From the owner's perspective, however, the timing was premature for a move to larger quarters because of lease commitments coupled with the uncertainties of a sluggish economy.

The implications of this apparent need for more space and the constraints of financial and economic realities were to surface time and time again during Best Image's work. However, the realities of the situation (we want to move/ we can't move) actually served to strengthen the teamwork between the owner and staff.

Once the staff had finished identifying the strengths, weaknesses and opportunities, the owner proceeded to put the group's work into context with the long-term vision and strategy which he had developed earlier for dealing with the space issue. Without going into specifics or actually showing the vision or strategy for facilities, the owner was able to explain that his long-term vision and strategy did include expanding the shop space by at least 250 square feet, and that during the coming months he would be working on several options to achieve that goal. By approaching the issue in this manner, not only did he validate and give importance to the work that the group had just finished, but, even more importantly, he was able to ensure involvement and support from his staff in looking for innovative ways of dealing with the space limitations.

In considering their weaknesses and opportunities, Best Image recognized three categories of action:

- weaknesses and opportunities which could be addressed *immediately* by either the owner or designated staff, such as new signs to make them more visible to customers,

- weaknesses and opportunities which could be addressed in the *short-term* future (next several months) as part of Phase IV of The MNM Process, such as the ventilation and noise issues, and

- weaknesses and opportunities which could only be addressed on a *long-term* basis (over many months) as part of the long-term vision and strategy, such as the issue of cramped working space.

By focusing on the weaknesses and opportunities and dividing them into a time-based action plan, two important steps were taken to ensure the success of The MNM Process. First, it demonstrated to the staff that their ideas and work were being taken seriously and *would* be put to use as part of an overall plan. Second, by including the staff in all of these discussions, the owner was able to secure a level of commitment for implementing the corrective action that would not have been obtained had he simply managed by decree.

Recommendations for Implementation

Assuming, as the old saying goes, you have done your homework, your first session as facilitator should go very smoothly. Remember that this process is as new for your staff as it was for you *before* you read this book, so you should have very little difficulty in carrying the day!

Best Image Printing – Facilities

Strengths:

1. *Good location and accessible*	8. *Air conditioned, good heating system*
2. *Good parking*	
3. *Clean*	9. *Accessible for delivery, both in and out*
4. *Bright with good lighting*	
5. *Pleasant interior*	10. *Rugs provide comfort for standing*
6. *Professional appearance*	11. *Kitchen area for staff*
7. *Ample customer area*	12. *No smoking policy*

Weaknesses:

1. *Cramped working space*
   - *aisle space particularly*
   - *bindery area, particularly when*

Opportunities Offered by Weaknesses:

1. *Acquiring more space would:*
   a. *make us more efficient, particularly in the bindery*

<table>
<tr><td>

   collating, can be problem
- *pressroom is OK*
- *counter space for customers is a problem at times*
- *computer area can be a problem with two or more people in it*

</td><td>

b. *help the work flow*
c. *reduce errors, i.e. the high-speed copying area*
d. *expansion and growth potential*
e. *create more attractive, useful and conducive work space for customers*
f. *improve staff sense of well being, less stress, quality of work life*

</td></tr>
<tr><td>

2. *Noise level from all machines*

</td><td>

2. *Reducing noise would:*
   a. *make it easier to maintain phone conversations for better service; relaxed, courteous, and clearer information*
   b. *reduce distractions at the counter*

</td></tr>
<tr><td>

3. *Not enough storage space*

</td><td>

3. *More storage space would facilitate organizing jobs*

</td></tr>
<tr><td>

4. *Customers see competition's store first*

</td><td>

4. *With respect to the competition's store – we should look into ways of making us more visible and seen first by the potential customer, i.e. better signs, etc.*

</td></tr>
<tr><td>

5. *Ventilation and air quality poor*

</td><td>

5. *Air quality could be improved by fans or air cleaning systems, such as filters, deionizers, etc.*

</td></tr>
<tr><td>

6. *Lack of break area*

</td><td>

6. *A break area would reduce stress by providing a place for a real break, and would provide a common place for staff to socialize*

</td></tr>
<tr><td>

7. *Lighting in pressroom area is not wonderful*

</td><td>

7. *Better lighting in pressroom would:*
   a. *increase efficiency*
   b. *reduce errors*
   c. *reduce color problems*
   d. *relieve eye strain*

</td></tr>
<tr><td>

8. *Space is maxed out for expansion*

</td><td>

8. *With more extra space we could expand into new areas of service*

</td></tr>
</table>

Immediate action: 4, 7
Short-term action: 2, 5, 6
Long-term action: 1, 3, 6, 8

Session 2
EQUIPMENT

Goals and Objectives

Your goal is to utilize your staff's input to examine your current equipment and its capabilities relative to the ideal vision for equipment you developed in Chapter 7.

Your specific objectives will be to first examine the current strengths and weaknesses of your existing equipment, and then explore the opportunities for these weaknesses, as was done in Session 1.

Preparatory Information, Learning or Action

The approach that you will take in this session will be quite similar to that of Session 1. Again, prior to the meeting you will want to review your vision and strategy statements for equipment which you developed in Chapters 7 and 9. Equipment is one area where staff can have tremendous input, particularly as it relates to the productivity and quality of their area. What they generally do not understand, of course, are the financial and economic aspects of buying and replacing equipment. While it is not necessary to go into these financial aspects in detail, a basic understanding as to initial costs, repair costs and replacement costs can help considerably in building account-ability and responsibility for equipment maintenance and preventing un-necessary breakdowns. An explanation of profit centers will help your staff understand why they can't have every piece of equipment they want and why you choose to invest in certain equipment.

Prior to this meeting you should ask your staff to take some time to prepare a list of their perception of the strengths, weaknesses and opportunities of the existing equipment, particularly the equipment in their area. Now that they have an idea of what the meetings will be like, you should find that the level of input will increase both in quantity and quality.

Case Study Discussion and Analysis

Like any business, Best Image has numerous equipment problems—some major, many minor—and lots of issues that fall into the nuisance category. Unlike some of the other components of a business, the opportunities generated in this session generally come down to a matter of hard economics: does it make sense to buy the equipment or not. One of the side benefits of The MNM Process is that it allows your staff to see alternative solutions to the immediate conclusions they are so quick to offer ("we need a new one" or "we should buy an another one"). By involving your staff in the basics of shop equipment economics, the understanding that a replacement or additional piece of equipment is simply not possible at the present time should lead to a more accepting and contented staff, and often will lead to useful innovation. Necessity coupled with *understanding*—not frustration— is the mother of invention.

It is important to emphasize that the understanding gained during a particular session will continue long after that session is completed. In the case of Best Image, the work developed in this session served to stimulate continuing thought and good suggestions concerning equipment from that session forward. Even several months after the meeting, staff members continued to have innovative ideas regarding equipment weaknesses identified there.

Towards the end of this session the owner introduced the vision and strategy for equipment that he had put together earlier. The staff was able to see that much of the work they had done was in alignment with the owner's ideas (for example, the addition of another high-speed copier). It also provided a good opportunity for the owner to introduce some new ideas, such as the implementation of an equipment failure monitoring system, the need for a staff-developed preventive maintenance system, and the concept of an emergency equipment breakdown contingency plan. By introducing his ideas at the same time the staff was introducing *their* ideas, the sense of staff acting in partnership with the owner was strengthened, and all participants left the meeting with a much greater sense of ownership and commitment for *all* ideas expressed, not just for their own.

Recommendations for Implementation

In this session, perhaps more so than in any other, your role as listener is critical. As owner, no one knows better than you the frustration of making do with less than optimum equipment—unless, of course, it's your staff! So listen, ask questions and gently probe for the real source of the problem. Often times something simple like increasing the wattage of a light source or adding a new light fixture can change an attitude of "it's the equipment's fault" to one of "the equipment seems to be working much better now."

It is quite likely that this session will generate many positive courses of action that can be taken to improve your equipment situation. It is important, therefore, that you take the time to break them down into a three-fold, time-based plan of immediate, short-term, and long-term action, as was shown in Session 1. This action plan should be formally written up and included in the minutes. It will be referred to frequently during the coming weeks, and will become one of the focus points of Phase IV.

Best Image Printing – Equipment

Strengths

1. *All equipment is new or fairly new and essentially state-of-the-art*
2. *Computers are reliable*
3. *Capable of producing quality products*
4. *Capable of meeting most of the job requirements*
5. *Minor equipment is replaced when it wears out*

Strengths (continued):

6. *Most equipment is reliable considering the amount of use it gets*
7. *Computers offer a strategic business advantage*
8. *Equipment is generally well maintained and as a result the products and copies are good*
9. *Cutter is safe to operate*
10. *Equipment in general is safe*

Weaknesses

1. *The high-speed copier is down too often and has no backup*
2. *Platemaker jams frequently, slowing production*
3. *Cutter is eccentric, doesn't always cut straight. Is this a design problem? Also, the cutter is sort of wimpy for some of the jobs we do. It wastes paper, and causes errors which domino or compound through the system, causing jobs to be redone*
4. *Light table is inadequate—too small and wimpy.*
5. *Collator is too small, both in terms of number of sheets it can handle at one time as well as sheet size; can be a bottleneck*
6. *Drill is difficult to align and is wimpy*
7. *Shop could use another spiral binder*
8. *Shop could use an envelope feeder for press*
9. *Press could use a dampener*
10. *Need a flat file for plates and negatives*
11. *Need wider shelves for storing mechanicals*
12. *Need inventory of larger envelopes and bags*
13. *Some equipment does not have competent service available*

Opportunities Offered by Weaknesses:

1. *A new high-speed copier would eliminate downtime and open up new service capabilities; it could reassure old customers and get new ones*
2. *We should try to find competent service for the camera; in the future, purchase of new equipment should be considered in terms of service available as well as performance*
3. *See opportunities listed for 2. above*
4. *Where would we put a larger light table? Also, see 6. below*
5. *See opportunities listed for 4; perhaps invest in booklet maker; also, see 6. below*
6. *Additional equipment must result in either a) increased sales, b) new product or service opportunities, c) improved quality, or d) reduction in downtime or rework.*
7. *See 6. above*
8. *See 6. above*
9. *Do cost analysis*
10. *Do cost analysis; also, see 6. above*
11. *Use plywood shelf extenders; do cost analysis of new unit*
12. *Do cost analysis*
13. *Investigate other service sources*

Immediate Action: 2, 3, 4, 13
Short-term Action: 1, 5, 6, 9, 10, 11, 12
Long-term Action: 5, 7, 8

Session 3
PRODUCTS & SERVICES

Goals and Objectives

In this session you and your staff will conduct a comprehensive and in-depth analysis of your current products and services before comparing it to the ideal vision you developed earlier. This analysis will begin with an examination of current strengths and weaknesses, and then explore the opportunities for these weaknesses, as you did in the two previous sessions.

Preparatory Information, Learning or Action

Services and products are a topic on which your staff will have much to contribute. As owner you want to make sure you allow enough time for each of your staff to contribute. This is one area where the collective whole will be much greater than the sum of all the pieces. If you are patient and skillful, the understanding that can come from piecing together their various contributions concerning products and services can be extremely valuable.

Case Study Discussion and Analysis

By this meeting, Best Image's staff had become very involved in The MNM Process, and, as can be seen in the list of perceived opportunities, had already started coming forward with numerous positive and innovative solutions to perceived weakness and problems. Another important change that began to surface (as evidenced in Opportunities 1d, 1e, 1f, 3b, 6, 7b and 10) was the fact that the staff was beginning to recognize and articulate important reasons for them working more closely together as a team. If you consider that these statements were being offered spontaneously as solutions to company problems which *they* had identified, as opposed to staff members simply parrotting company policies or doctrine, it is obvious that the process was beginning to have an effect.

Perhaps the most interesting thing about this session, however, comes from a comparison of the owner's vision and strategy for products and services with the work the staff did in this session. Certainly the opportunities that the staff perceived in their analysis of products and services are in line with the owner's vision and articulated desire for expanding and increasing printing and copying capabilities. However, if you look at the owner's strategy, it bears little resemblance to the strategies for improvement recognized by the staff. Whereas the owner's strategy focused primarily on *adding equipment and personnel,* the staff focused on *better utilization of existing systems* and *developing teamwork* to increase productivity and satisfy customers. The important point here is that implementing either of these two approaches on their own can lead to expanded and increased printing capabilities, but implementing them *together* will prove exceptional.

Recognizing the importance of the synergy that had developed in this session, Best Image's owner was most anxious to capitalize on these unanticipated ideas and energy. Accordingly, a considerable amount of time was devoted to working out an implementation strategy. While some of the ideas were put off to become part of the work of Phase IV, many were able to be implemented immediately.

Recommendations for Implementation

There is, of course, no way of predicting what ideas or suggestions will come to light during The MNM Process. It's a very spontaneous process, and this is the primary reason it works. As facilitator, you should not be discouraged if a particular meeting does not generate the quality or quantity of ideas or input that you had hoped for. Like individual creativity, group synergy cannot be forced to happen. It *can* be encouraged, but definitely not demanded.

The important thing to keep in mind is that when synergy does occur, as it did for Best Image in this session, you make the most of it. If towards the end of a session, you find yourself looking at a long list of promising opportunities, strike while the synergy is sizzling and act immediately! Your opportunity, now, is to put on your leader hat and ask for volunteers to take on the responsibility of following through with the opportunity. Management by delegation in action!

Best Image Printing – Products & Services

Strengths

1. *Good, high quality typesetting service which is priced competitively*
2. *Wide variety of services*
3. *High quality service and products*
4. *Staff tries to accommodate all reasonable customer requests; occasionally unreasonable requests, too.*
5. *Customers are offered best price and given options for their benefit*
6. *Offer good advice, guidance, technical assistance*
7. *Take a lot of time serving customers*
8. *Camera and fax offer extra service*
9. *Can do in-house proofing*
10. *Laminating is a good service*
11. *Free pads build customer allegiance*
12. *Will do rework cheerfully*
13. *Donate printing to regular non-profit customers*
14. *Sensitive to customer deadlines*
15. *Willing to take on jobs requiring subcontracts*
16. *Knowledge of customers' strengths and weaknesses*

Weaknesses	*Opportunities Offered by Weaknesses*
1. Problem in meeting some promised deadlines	1. a. Work on establishing better rapport with customers as pertains to deadlines b. Analyze deadline failures to develop corrective action c. Be realistic in scheduling d. Provide better communication between internal departments e. Provide more cross training/ understanding of other departments f. Identify multi-task jobs so that they don't come as a surprise
2. Charge for certain services (i.e. resumes) considered high; prices not competitive in certain areas	2. a. Do some research on competition b. Analyze best profit centers vs. competitive prices c. Use less expensive specialty printers
3. Errors during busy time periods throw system in chaos; no margin to accommodate errors in system during busy periods.	3. a. Be aware of the fact that busy time equals more errors b. Develop "early warning system" or "daily chaos potential meter"
4. Lack of formal proofing policy/ procedure/guidelines, including deadline policies	4. a. Take a look at developing an improved proofing form for customer b. Develop rescheduling policy for customers who fail to proof on time
5. No pamphlets to offer guidance to customers on helpful hints on how to prepare work for shop	5. a. Have an open house b. Offer workshops/educational programs
6. Accommodating unreasonable requests, i.e., deadlines	6. a. Closer communication between front desk and print dept. b. Schedule jobs immediately upon taking them c. Bright orange sticker on schedule board for problematic jobs
7. Lack of policy/statement to educate customers, particularly new customers, about deadlines	7. a. Be more conscientious in getting **real** deadlines from the customer b. Get jobs on the board immediately c. Notify customers as soon as it is obvious that you may not meet the deadline; eliminate surprises d. Avoid unrealistic promises
8. Lack of education of the customers as to BI actual services, i.e., <u>not</u> a quick copy company	8. a. Continue to educate customers on a daily basis
9. Lack of advertising of BI real strengths, what BI can really do	9. a. Educate people as to what BI can really do

10. *Not fully utilizing existing person-nel/equipment. Could use better team approaches*

    b. *Internal display of samples of work; binders with samples*

10. a. *In-house orientation/training to familiarize employees with what goes on in other departments/ areas*

    b. *Cross-training - each staff person should consider each piece of equipment in terms of the following:*
      1. *Constantly use equipment*
      2. *Periodically use equipment*
      3. *Would use equipment if I knew how, and could make operation run more smoothly*

11. *Don't really offer pick-up and delivery*

11. *Free pick-up and delivery would entice customers to use us*

Immediate action: 1a, 1c, 1d, 1f, 2a, 2c, 3a, 3b, 4a, 4b, 6a-c, 7a-d, 8a, 9a, 10a
Short-term action: 1b, 1d, 1e, 2a, 2b, 5a, 8a, 9a, 9b, 10b, 11
Long-term action: 1e, 5b, 8a, 9a

Session 4
VENDORS

Goals and Objectives

The goal of Session 4 focuses on a critical but often neglected area of every business: your vendor relationships and how you can improve them. Assuming your business is typical, you will probably find the analysis of the strengths and weaknesses of your vendors easy to define, but the opportunities rather difficult to grasp.

Preparatory Information, Learning and Action

It is quite likely that you will find this session does not stimulate staff involvement to the extent that the previous sessions have, and you may have to take a more active role in order to keep the session going. The reason, of course, is that in most small businesses the owner maintains vendor contact, not the staff.

If you think this may be the case, you might want to prepare a list of questions like these to prompt discussion.

    – Are you aware of any problems we may be having with any of our paper vendors?

- Considering the equipment that you use, have you experienced repeated problems that you think might be eliminated if we had a different service contract?
- Are you aware of any new suppliers in the area that we might want to try?
- We seem to be having a real problem with XYZ Graphic Supplies in terms of getting our orders on time. Does anyone have any suggestions as to how we can bring them around?

Case Study Discussion and Analysis

Prior to this session, the staff of Best Image had not given much thought to any vendor relationship. Consequently, input was limited and not very sophisticated. Nevertheless, the input did serve the purpose of starting the thought process as to what might be done to improve this aspect of the business.

Once the staff's input was completed, the shop owner introduced his 12-month vision and preliminary strategy for improving the vendor situation. Even though the staff's input had been limited, it was very much in alignment with the owner's vision and strategy. Consequently, it was easy to develop interest among the staff in thinking about and searching for ways and ideas of implementing the strategy he had conceived.

Recommendations for Implementation

By now your skill as a facilitator should be developing nicely. It's probably time to start focusing on other tools and approaches which might be useful in nurturing your staff's development. An option to consider for sessions that are not likely to generate as much input as others (such as this one), is to prepare relevant concepts or pieces of learning that you could introduce and discuss with your staff whenever the timing is appropriate. These could include internal customers, total quality or win/win concepts in customer or vendor relationships. When introduced in 20 or 30 minute bites, these concepts can serve to stimulate relevant dialogue among your staff, which, over several months, will add up to a significant amount of learning.

The value of win/win business relationships is an concept you can introduce in this session if you have time. Most of your staff probably already has an understanding of the difference between win/win and win/lose in their personal relationships, but may never have considered the business applications of the concept.

Basically, win/win means that all parties benefit in a positive manner (when I win, you also win) because a solution has been reached which makes everyone happy. A win/lose outcome to a problem means that in order for one side to benefit, the other cannot. An interesting book you might read and share with your staff on the topic is *The Win/Win Way* by Lucy Beale and Rick Fields.

Vendors offer a good way of introducing and discussing the win/win concept. By focusing as a team on your various vendors, the staff can debate whether or not they think certain vendors practice win/win or win/lose business approaches. This open discussion approach will lead to greater understanding of the concepts than if you were to simply present definitions. It also allows your staff to express how uncomfortable *they* feel when a vendor assumes a win/lose approach (with them as loser), and then explore and brainstorm ways in which win/win actions could be encouraged and nurtured.

The concept of win/win is the same whether we are talking vendors, external customers, or internal customers, so without ever focusing on the staff itself, the win/win concept is integrated into their understanding. By introducing and exploring the concept in the context of your vendors, it should only be a short time before your staff will start applying the concept among themselves as internal customers.

Best Image Printing – Vendors

Strengths

1. *Good network overall*
2. *Great ink supplier*
3. *Most are product knowledge-able*
4. *Paper availability fairly good*
5. *Good service for press*
6. *Good computer supplies*
7. *Have choices*

Weaknesses

1. *Paper companies*
   a. *Ship wrong materials*
   b. *Ship wrong amounts*
   c. *Invoices inaccurate*

2. *Service on camera is poor*

Opportunities Offered by Weaknesses

1. a. *Catch errors as they come in the door; check orders immediately*
   b. *Keep accurate records of errors and continue to keep company informed*
   c. *Order paper as much in advance as possible*
   d. *Educate paper companies as to better methods on ordering papers*
   e. *Keep daily order sheet for each of the three companies and once a month send a sheet to their management showing errors vs. acceptable orders*

2. *Contact manufacturer to notify them of the problems we are having and see if there are any other firms*

3. *Hard to find competent service on some equipment*

4. *Few sources for recycled paper; suppliers aren't interested yet*

in our area which might provide service

3. *Begin working to find service before needed; anticipate problems; be pro-active about weaknesses*

4.
   a. *Keep good records of people that would want, could use or prefer recycled paper*
   b. *Possibly poll customers for interest; start a "petition"*
   c. *Investigate sources from national pro-ecology organizations*
   d. *How big is this market? Should it be promoted at the franchisor level?*

Immediate action: 1a, 1e, 2, 3, 4c, 4d
Short-term action: 1b, 1c, 1d, 4a, 4b

Session 5
CUSTOMERS

Goals and Objectives

The goal of this session is to use the objective vision of your staff to develop a clear understanding of your existing customer base. As with products and services, you should find that your staff has an incredible wealth of information to offer relative to customers' strengths and weaknesses and will be very forthcoming in suggesting opportunities for improving the weaknesses.

Preparatory Information, Learning and Action

Customers are another area where it is more important for you as shop owner to do more listening than talking. As this session unfolds, you will likely find that your staff has considerably different impressions of your customers than you. This is only natural, as, again, you are too close to the situation. The more objective input your staff can offer you, the better. Keep in mind that often a customer will share information or confide approval/displeasure in your products or services more readily with a member of your staff than they might with you.

Preferences in Thinking Styles (Resource Tool A in The MNM Tool Box) presents an interesting concept which you might want to introduce to your staff before beginning this session on customers. Basically, the concept presents a simple, yet highly effective, way of understanding people by their preferred thinking and decision making styles. This concept can be particularly effective in dealing with various customer service issues. Many owners have also found that the concept can yield valuable insight when considering individual staff competencies as related to job function. Whether or not you perceive value in the concept is not critical to the implementation of this or any other part of The MNM Process. It is simply presented as a resource to be used at your discretion.

Case Study Discussion and Analysis

In examining the opportunities listed for customers, one cannot help but be impressed with the sensitivity and innovation expressed in some of the suggestions. Consider, for example, the opportunity suggested for weakness #4, customers bringing in poor mechanicals. Every printshop has experienced this problem, along with the resulting unpleasantness of extensive reworking, repricing, and generally disgruntled staff and customer.

The suggestion of offering workshops aimed at enabling customers to prepare better mechanicals offers great possibilities and illustrates perfectly the turning of a negative into a positive. It is not difficult to envision the news release announcing these workshops:

> *Best Image Printing offers three FREE evening workshops for office personnel responsible for company printing needs ... in addition to important tips on how to assure a professional, quality look, let us show you eight easy tricks of the trade that can save you BIG dollars on every printing job you ever do ... Call and make a reservation now! Your dinner time? Don't worry! ... hors d'oeuvres and refreshments will be served!*

A classic case of win/win. No amount of advertising could ever equal the kind of good will and long-term loyalty that an event like this could generate. And let your staff plan and execute the event! After all, it was their idea!

It is interesting to compare the staff-generated opportunities for customers with the vision and strategy for customers developed by the owner. Certainly there is a lot of alignment between them, but perhaps the most interesting observation is the way the staff was able to come up with viable and easily implemented strategies to achieve some of the same vision objectives that the owner had labored over. Best Image's owner has a very valuable asset in the collective thinking of his staff.

Recommendations for Implementation

This session will probably take more than one meeting period, especially if you introduce Preferences in Thinking Styles (Resource Tool A). If you do decide to introduce the Preferences material, try to keep it simple. There is ample documentation available for how and why these concepts work, and the references listed offer good introductory follow-up material for the exceptionally curious. My experience has been that one hour's time is quite ample to get the important points across. The concept is easily grasped by most people, and your staff should be able to put the concepts into action right away.

Best Image Printing – Customers

Strengths

1. Are willing to be partners in developing their work
2. Broad base of customers
3. Repeat, loyal customers; send referrals
4. Most pay as scheduled
5. Customers are not those greatly affected by recession
6. Most are understanding with respect to missed deadlines, errors, etc.

Weaknesses

1. Some can be very difficult and demanding

2. New customers can be difficult

3. Could use more customers

Opportunities Offered by Weaknesses

1. More cross-training will enable all staff to:
   a. Explain problems to customer's satisfaction
   b. Be sensitive to customer's displeasure **early enough** to do something about it
   c. Be sensitive to acknowledging waiting customers
   d. Keep smiling!
   e. Have uniform policy for dealing with customer's errors
   f. Be sensitive to right-brained customers' lack of attention to detail
   g. **ASSUME NOTHING!** Ask more questions; double check inconsistencies

2. a. See 1 a-g
   b. Impress on them the reality and need for real deadlines; try to find out the real deadline
   c. Make a good impression; make an extra effort to be helpful
   d. No false promises!

3. a. Continue present approach
   b. Investigate other modes of advertising
   c. Always ask new customers how they heard of us
   d. Improve direct mail list

4. *Many bring in poor mechanicals*

    4. a. *Workshops – maybe target specific groups such as designers and see how that goes; then maybe do one for the general public; show examples of good and bad work*

       b. *Give customers a better understanding about what their mechanicals will produce*

5. *Computer owners take advantage of BI*

    5. a. *Small %, but big problem!*

       b. *Prepare a policy statement to hand out concerning using/ reworking customers disks*

6. *Why do we lose customers? Dissatisfied customers can cost a lot of business.*

    6. a. ***DEADLINES AREN'T MET***

       b. *Final price higher than estimate*

       c. *First and second time customers; send card/letter requesting their evaluation of products and services*

       d. *Person dealing with left company; follow-up needed*

       e. *Owner is designated complaint/ potential lost customer person; we need to utilize appropriate action in this area as soon as it is obvious that there is a potential problem*

       f. *Discuss mistakes and use them to create more communication among ourselves and create better customer relations*

7. *Some customers come to expect special favors and consideration*

    7. a. *Give these people **deadlines***

       b. *Educate these customers as to company policies; particularly with respect to scheduling*

       c. *Be clear in stating policy to customers who are working with graphic designers and try to go direct; also, graphic designers **do** get priority in scheduling*

8. *Some are slow in returning correct- ed proofs*

    8. a. *Appraise customers of printing schedule relative to return of proofs*

       b. *Our policy is clear; but we need to make our customers more aware and then enforce it*

Immediate action: 2b, 2c, 2d, 3a, 3c, 4b, 5, 6a, 6b, 6d, 6e, 6f, 7a, 7c, 8a, 8b
Short-term action: 1, 2a, 3b, 3d, 4a, 6c, 7b

Session 6
COMPETITION

Goals and Objectives

The goal of this session is to take stock of your existing competition as it relates to your operation, first by considering their known strengths and weaknesses, and then by discovering how their weaknesses might translate into opportunities for your company.

Preparatory Information, Learning and Action

How to deal effectively with competition is an aspect of business which triggers a variety of opinions. Some companies completely ignore competition and quietly go about their business; others spend a major portion of their advertising dollars in presenting good reasons why their services or products are better.

Competition is *not* a major focus of The MNM Process. Instead, the overriding goal is to develop your company into a vibrant, innovative organization which is so closely attuned to the marketplace and to your customers' wants and needs that competition will have little effect. Accepting the challenge of this goal will lead to long-term improvement. However, for the short-term, an understanding of how your products, services and price structure measure up to those of your competitors is simply good, basic business strategy.

In exploring with your staff the issue of competition, you will probably have to exercise more of a leadership role than you had when dealing with other topics. While *you* may give a lot of thought to your competition, it is not a high-priority topic for your staff. Nevertheless, collectively they probably have considerable relevant information to offer. Best Image Printing may offer some ideas on how to approach your own session on competition. Some additional suggestions are presented in the analysis.

Case Study Discussion and Analysis

What became obvious to Best Image's owner by the time the staff had finished the session, was that the issue was more a matter of marketing and advertising than of competition. Relative to their competition, Best Image was already receiving high marks in most categories. As someone pointed out, their biggest problem was simply that not enough of their potential customer base *knew* about their capabilities. The session indicated that the area needing work was in more closely defining the product and service niche of Best Image relative to the other printing companies in town, and then letting the business community know about it.

The owner's vision and strategy for competition was in close alignment with the results of this session. In comparing the staff's work with the owner's vision and strategy, the staff saw that they had provided input on critical issues previously recognized by the owner. At the end of this session the staff had an increased awareness of their relationship to the competition, and the type of information which would be useful for them to know.

Recommendations for Implementation

One way of stimulating greater input in this session on competition is to frame several key questions before beginning which can be written out and taped to the wall. A good place to begin looking for some ideas for questions would be the vision and strategy for competition which you developed earlier and also the minutes of the session on products and services. For example, if we were to use Best Image's vision and strategy for competition, we might generate questions similar to those presented below to get the discussion going.

- We need to know more about how our pricing stacks up to the other shops in the area. Have any of you heard any comments from our customers or other sources that would suggest we are out of line, either high or low?

- Lately we seem to be seeing a decrease in our high-speed copying. Any ideas as to what might be the reason?

- There is probably a lot our customers would be willing to share with us about our competition. Any suggestions as to how we might systematically go about getting this information without appearing too nosey and putting them on the spot?

Best Image Printing – Competition

Strengths

1. *Our parking is better than at shops in town*
2. *Numerous customers have said that our turn-around times are faster*
3. *People seem to appreciate our willingness to help them and offer ideas for saving them money*
4. *Long-time customers give us referrals*
5. *Perceived by business community as offering full-service*
6. *Customers like our computer design capabilities and how quickly we can turn their ideas into a finished product*
7. *The word about our quality seems to be getting around, and it also seems to be getting much more important to the customer*
8. *Customers say we're easier to deal with*

Weaknesses	Opportunities Offered by Weaknesses
1. Other places charge less for resumes	1. a. Investigate what other shops are charging and what is included in their service b. Our resume package is a quality-based product which has resulted (according to our customers) in a high percentage of interviews. Is this something that we could capitalize on, in our advertising or pricing over the phone? Many people do not realize the difference that a professional resume can make in getting that interview
2. Several customers have gone over to a competitor who recently got a color copier	2. a. Great Prints has a new color copier and incredibly low prices to get people in the door b. Getting a color copier would offer another service to our customers, and we would probably get some new ones
3. We don't do much work for the medical or legal professions, and have lost some of those customers. Why?	3. a. Could do a survey of this group's needs b. Some of those customers have switched to continuous forms which they buy from other places; we need to let all customers know we can do these, too
4. People have complained about how long they have had to stand in our shop before being waited on	4. a. Provide magazines and chairs, even tho we don't have much space b. Acknowledge their presence as often as needed until we can wait on them
5. Some customers have said they can get two-color jobs faster elsewhere	5. a. Some of our competition make promises they can't keep. Make sure customers know we keep ours b. Get another two-color press c. Promote "we keep our promises" in ads
6. Several customers have complained that they have difficulty in getting the information they need	6. a. Do some work in left/right brain styles so we can read customers more easily
7. We don't have any recycled paper in stock and people ask for it	7. a. Investigate sources and have something on hand all the time that is reasonably priced b. Know about other available papers so can offer when needed c. Keep discussing with paper companies so they'll increase their in-

			ventory
8.	*People don't know about us*	8.	a. *Find new ways of advertising*
			b. *Offer discount to customers who refer a new customer*
			c. *Get written about in local business magazines or newspaper*
9.	*Don't offer pick-up and delivery*	9.	*Pick up and delivery would get more customers*

Immediate action: 1a, 3b, 4a, 4b, 5a, 7a, 7b, 8b, 9
Short-term action: 1b, 2b, 3a, 5c, 6, 7c, 8a, 8c
Long-term action: 5b

Session 7
MARKETING & SALES

Goals and Objectives

The goal of this session is to consider your existing marketing and sales position. As in previous sessions, the objectives are to obtain your staff's input on strengths and weaknesses, and then look at the opportunities offered by the weaknesses.

Preparatory Information, Learning and Action

At first consideration, you might think marketing and sales is an area in which your staff wouldn't have much input. Like many printshops, you probably don't have a designated marketing person or official sales rep and, instead, see this area as totally your responsibility. If you think about it, though, every day each person on your staff is sending signals to and receiving signals from your customers, either directly or indirectly, in the form of the products and services they provide. In this sense they are *all* involved in your company's marketing and sales effort and on a daily basis are having a major impact on your overall marketing strategy.

Certainly a long-term marketing strategy is important, such as adding five new market segments to your customer base over the next 12 months. Yet, if your staff does not understand *their* role and impact on your short-term marketing and sales efforts, it's possible that your existing customer base could be eroding as fast as new customers are being added! Before we consider the best way of bringing these concepts into your staff's awareness, take a look at how Best Image approached the issue.

Case Study and Analysis

In considering Best Image's minutes, two observations stand out. First, the staff *did* express considerable interest in the area of sales and marketing and had some very relevant and objective questions to ask as to why certain things were and weren't being done. Second, it is obvious from the way the questions and the suggested opportunities are phrased that the staff feels its role in The MNM Process is genuine, and that their comments and input are being taken seriously. The opportunities show that the staff is perhaps more aware of the day-to-day influence of their performance on the marketing effort than the owner might have thought.

By soliciting the staff's input first, it makes the introduction of the owner's vision and strategy for marketing and sales much easier. Because of the way in which the session unfolded, it actually served to set-up the introduction of the owner's vision and strategy and permitted a much higher and quicker degree of ownership than might have otherwise been possible.

Recommendations for Implementation

It is hard to predict how this session will develop for your group. They may have a lot of input, such as the Best Image staff, or they may be hesitant. The reason is primarily the subject matter, and many of your staff might not see, at first, their personal connection to the topic of marketing and sales.

It might be useful if you were to again develop ahead of time some questions aimed at getting the discussion going or resuscitating it when it begins to lag. As in Session 6, your vision and strategy is a good place to look for ideas for leading questions. Here are some sample questions developed from Best Image's vision and preliminary strategy.

- We need to expand our customer base during the coming year, can you think of any market segments that we are not serving that we might want to look at?

- Have you gotten any feedback from customers as to whether our marketing and advertising strategy is effective?

- Do any of you see any new opportunities in terms of marketing that we might want to try?

- How does our marketing and advertising stack up when compared to our competition?

Best Image Printing – Marketing & Sales

Strengths

1. *National marketing program through franchise*	2. *Free pads promote good will*
	3. *Yellow pages ad is large and*

Strengths (continued)
        well placed
    4. *We get more customers because
        of the charity work we do*
    5. *With our new sign we have
        greater visibility*

6. *More people are using our fax
    service*
7. *Direct mail pieces usually bring in
    new business*

Weaknesses

1. *Some national materials is not
    relevant for our area*
2. *Competition uses radio more than
    we do*

3. *Our last mailing piece generated a
    poor response; what was wrong?
    They have always worked before*

4. *A few customers have commented
    that the phones were always busy
    and then when they did get
    through, they got put on hold*

5. *Our customers don't know every-
    thing we can do*

6. *We should have been in the trade
    show at the convention center last
    week*
7. *Our price list is old*

Opportunities Offered by Weaknesses

1. *We can discuss the poor pieces as a
    group and modify them as needed*
2. *Franchisor's radio campaign uses
    stations with few listeners; investi-
    gate using local radio*
3. a. *Think more about timing of
        mailing*
    b. *Update mailing list on a regular
        basis; ask current customers if
        they want to be on our mailing
        list*
    c. *Develop our own pieces to use in
        addition to franchisor's*
    d. *Hire an ad agency or designer to
        do our pieces*
4. a. *Investigate cost of another line*
    b. *Personal calls at noon are
        increasing; can we police
        ourselves or should we have a
        formal policy?*
    c. *Be more aware of our telephone
        manners and attitude; every call
        is a mini-ad for BI*
5. a. *Prepare a marketing piece to put
        in with finished jobs that lists all
        our services*
    b *Do a mailer that lists all services
        and use it several times a year*
    c. *Send out a newsletter which
        focuses on all the services BI
        offers and hints on preparing
        mechanicals, etc.*
    d. *Call on potential customers and
        tell them what we do*
6. *We have never done a trade show;
    maybe we should try one; check the
    possibilities*
7. *Redo the price list and prepare a
    mini version listing our services to
    give to customers*

*Immediate action: 4a-c, 5a, 7
Short-term action: 1, 2, 3a-d, 5b, 5c, 5d
Long-term action: 5d, 6*

Session 8
GENERAL ECONOMIC OUTLOOK

Goals and Objectives

The goal of this session is take a look at the prevailing general economic climate and outlook in terms of how it will impact your business both in the present and in the foreseeable future. To achieve this goal we will again look at perceived strengths and weaknesses of the economy, and then proceed to convert these weaknesses into opportunities.

Preparatory Information, Learning and Action

An old adage which occasionally crops up on office walls offers the following wisdom, "There are three types of people: those who make things happen, those who watch things happen, and those who wonder what happened!" There is a lot of truth in this statement, and with a little rewording it becomes quite relevant to our discussion about printing businesses and the economy: those businesses that understand what's happening, those businesses that watch what's happening, and those businesses that wonder what happened.

It is extremely hard these days to find much that economists and business gurus can agree on, except, perhaps, that the future will unquestionably be a roller-coaster ride of change. The problem is that as the number and complexity of economic variables increase, it becomes more difficult to predict the outcome of any individual economic fluctuation. But while *prediction may be impossible, understanding* of events *is possible.* And with understanding, it is also possible for a business to respond in more appropriate ways to various economic events as they take place.

As any strategist would agree, the key to understanding a situation and making the right move is in having the most accurate and up-to-date information. This is true whether you are playing football, engaging in war, or running a business.

Every day your business is presented with innumerable signals and indications about the current status of the general economic climate. A primary receiver of such information is your staff. They are on the firing line and they are in constant contact with the customers and the work being produced. If encouraged and taught what to watch for, they can be a most valuable source of timely data for understanding current economic trends. Quite simply, just as two heads can be better than one, several sets of eyes and ears are better than the owner's alone. It is unfortunate, however, that few business owners take the time to utilize this resource. After all, they reason, *what could my staff possibly know or understand that I don't!*

This session will focus on nurturing your staff's ability to identify and report useful pieces of economic input. But first we are going to introduce a tool which you might find useful for developing initial staff awareness on this subject.

Strategic Futuring (Resource Tool B) is a powerful, yet simple-to-use process which enables a group of people to explore and discover together highly probable future outcomes for any given subject or question. The process utilizes consensus-based thinking to produce understanding which reflects the combined best thinking of the participating group. With this process, for example, it would be possible for you as facilitator to start with a central question, such as "How would a moderate recession affect our business?", and in the course of an hour develop a highly probable scenario in terms of how a recession would impact every facet of your business—customers, cost of supplies, marketing, personnel, etc. Since the scenario is based on the input of all your staff, *each person takes ownership in the potential outcome.* With this increased awareness and understanding, the significance of the information your staff receives daily from your customers takes on greater meaning.

Strategic Futuring is recommended for but not essential to the implementation of this session. Again, each of the tools and concepts presented in this book are suggestions only. *You* are the facilitator and the leader, and by this time should have a good sense of what methods will work best with your staff.

Case Study Discussion and Analysis

This session demonstrates clearly the value and need for constant monitoring of the business data that the staff is receiving. It also demonstrates effectively to the staff how data previously considered trivial can become very useful when put into an overall economic context.

Some owners might take the position that it is unnecessary for staff to be wasting their time like this in considering "the big picture," as that is management's role. This attitude is about as valid as a football coach who goes to great pains to get game films of the team's next opponent and never shows them to the team! No, The MNM Process would suggest that such understanding not only provides for a more aware and flexible organization, but also serves to add a new dimension of interest, understanding and meaning to your staff's work which will continue to serve the company in the weeks and months to come. Following a session like this, it is easy to see how the owner's vision and strategy for facilities, equipment, and marketing, etc. would take on much greater meaning for the staff. And, as we have discussed, the greater the staff's buy-in to a company's vision, the more successful that organization will be in achieving that vision.

Recommendations for Implementation

This session has been more general and outward looking than previous sessions, and in a sense, provides a good transition to Task II, which is intensely focused on your staff and in developing a self-managing team for your business.

As this is the last session in the "Snapshot In Time" part of The MNM Process, it might be appropriate, either at the close of this session or in a separate meeting, to give special recognition to your staff for reaching their first milestone. What that special touch might be is up to you, perhaps a nice dinner or holding the session in a different location. The important thing is to acknowledge the progress that has been made and lay the foundation for the Task 2 work which will follow.

Best Image Printing – Current Economic Outlook

Strengths

1. *Business continues to expand; new customers still coming in*
2. *Several manufacturing plants are expanding their operations*
3. *State-wide business appears stable*
4. *Many people still moving into state and finding work*
5. *Federal officials say recession unlikely*

Weaknesses

1. *Real estate seems to have stagnated; this sector of our business is off*

2. *Number of accounts over 60 days is up*

3. *Several big customers report their company is laying off workers, including people with seniority*

Opportunities Offered by Weaknesses

1. a. *Need to watch all accounts and listen to customers very carefully to see how different businesses are experiencing the economy*
   b. *May want to reduce our limits on charge accounts, particularly in certain sectors such as real estate*

2. a. *Monitor accounts weekly from now on; look for changes in historical payment pattern*
   b. *Develop better system of following-up on overdue accounts and implement it*

3. a. *Pay close attention to this kind of information; are there any patterns?*

4. Several customers now beginning to cut back on size of orders, and are opting for less expensive pieces
5. Increase in number of people calling about resumes
6. The downtown tourist area merchants association just reported a very poor year

b. Assuming the economy is slowing down, should we be looking at our customer base in terms of vulnerability to recession?
c. Actively seek to broaden our base of customers, and don't keep all our eggs in one basket
4. Showing customers ways in which they can save money should, ultimately, bring in more business
5. Expand our capability and advertising in this area
6. a. Assuming the fall-off in tourists this summer was not just due to poor weather or other factors, we might want to look at what percentage of our customers are dependent upon the local tourist economy and what potential customer segments are available in the area that are not related to tourism?
b. If the fall-off is real, make a sales pitch to the state tourist board?

Immediate action: 1a, 1b, 2a, 2b, 3a, 3b, 3c, 4, 5, 6a
Short-term action: 1a, 2a, 2b, 3a, 3b, 3c, 6b
Long-term action: 2a, 2b, 3c

In discussing the strengths and weaknesses of the economy, the group noted that there seemed to be conflicting signals. While on the surface things seemed fine, and certainly the official word and media where positive, at the customer level there were signs that all was not well. The group agreed that the situation should be closely watched and that perhaps the marketing strategy for the next six months should be reconsidered.

Summary

Session 8 concludes Task 1, the development of a "Snapshot In Time" of your business. You should now have an extremely accurate picture of your business as it presently exists. As owner, you may have been surprised by some of the observations that your staff made, and, perhaps, some of them were a little difficult to accept. We hope that's the case, as that was the primary intent of this part of the process: to see your business as others see it, warts and all!

CHAPTER 12

THE TASK 2 STAFF MEETINGS

In The MNM Team Building Process Task 2 staff meetings, your energy will be focused on developing your staff into a self-managing team. In reality, the team has been forming since you started the meetings that comprised Task 1, but we have purposely not mentioned the word team, let alone self-managing team. In the next six sessions we'll talk a lot about teams, but without using the term self-managing. Why? There is no need, as the self-managing part will simply happen. In a sense, a self-managing team is like an african violet—shining too much light on it may have unpleasant results.

Some of the sessions in Task 1 probably caused you to blink a few times as your staff got into the spirit of holding up a mirror to your alter ego—your business. Hopefully, it wasn't all that stressful, and you've become a stronger person for the experience! Now you have the opportunity to turn the tables a bit. Throughout this part of The MNM Process your staff is going to be looking into that same mirror, only this time they'll be looking at themselves! Your role here is threefold. You must still be the facilitator, and in addition you will play the roles of coach and part-time team member. The challenge continues!

There is a very important reason for not allowing the staff to look at themselves earlier in the process, and that's because it is important to allow time for the individual staff members to come together as a team and become comfortable with each other—and with you—in this new mode of open sharing and interaction. At this point, with the team spirit and trust that has built up over the last few months, your team is ready to take on the more demanding task of looking closely at themselves.

Each of the six sessions of Task 2 focuses on a particular aspect of the team building process.

Session 9:   Individual staff perceptions of how the business presently performs as a team.

Session 10:   Staff exploration using personal thoughts and ideas of the concept of what the ideal team for the business should be.

Session 11:   Identify and rank the Ten Key Characteristics of the Ideal Company Team.

Session 12:   Group exploration of the weakest areas of the Ten Key Characteristics that were identified in Session 11 and development of strategies for improving them.

Session 13:   Continued exploration of the weak areas identified in Session 11 and development of strategies for improving them.

Session 14:   Continued exploration of the weak areas identified in Session 11 and development of strategies for improving them.

Task 2 continues to use Best Image Printing as a case study for The MNM Process, and the format for presenting each session is similar to that used in Task 1 (goals and objectives, preparatory information, case study discussion and analysis, recommendations for conducting the sessions, and Best Image's minutes).

Session 9
HOW THE STAFF PERCEIVES THE EXISTING
COMPANY TEAM

Goals and Objectives

The goal of this session is for the staff to explore their perceptions of how the business is presently performing as a team. Specific objectives are for each staff member to articulate their perceptions individually, discuss possible relationships between them and learn to value each other's contributions.

Preparatory Information, Learning and Action

In this session you will use a technique called "Insight through Metaphor" to help your staff develop and articulate their perception of existing team performance. The technique is simple, enjoyable, and very effective. What you will do is ask each person to think for a few minutes and come up with an *animal, plant, machine, or other inanimate object* which they think most closely resembles the shop's team at the present time. Once they have done this, you will ask them to write *or* draw (it is most important to give this option) *in detail* how this animal, plant, or machine resembles the team. Each member of the staff will share their perceptions in a group discussion once everyone has finished.

The Insight through Metaphor technique is extremely useful for developing fresh and innovative perspectives on any subject. To use metaphor in considering a subject is to employ an entirely different set of thinking processes and skills than we would normally use when responding to a question. Generally, exploring a concept by metaphor will lead to an understanding which shows great insight and synthesis of numerous pieces of detail. The reason that you give the option of writing or drawing the answer is because some people think in words, while others think in pictures (see Resource Tool A).

You will probably find that the metaphors your staff produces are humorous, yet extremely accurate. Most importantly, however, this exercise will demonstrate that while each person may come up with a totally different metaphor, all of them are, in their own way, correct, as each captures something that the others didn't see. Thus, your staff will see (in a subtle or not so subtle way, depending how you as facilitator play it) that there can be great value and insight in a fellow staff person's perceptions and understanding even though they are considerably different than one's own.

Case Study Discussion and Analysis

As you can see, some of the Best Image staff's metaphors are funny and others quite serious, yet all offer powerful images and statements regarding team attributes. None of the metaphors are exactly alike, and although some expressed similar concepts, they did so from totally different perspectives. When the individual metaphors were written on the flip chart, seeing them together offered a very significant and forceful statement as to how the staff saw themselves as a team.

At this point in The MNM Process, the Best Image staff was already functioning fairly well together as a team, so the metaphors were virtually all positive. The exception to this was the owner, who was concerned about the times everyone was buzzing but accomplishing nothing (that's a typical owner concern!). But, as was pointed out in the meeting, even if the wheels were only spinning sometimes, at least they were spinning together!

Recommendations for Implementation

It may be that you can see the objectives and value of this session; yet it might seem so different from your normal approach to business that you feel somewhat hesitant in your ability to facilitate this work. Certainly this fear is valid; no one likes to look like a fool, particularly in front of their own staff. We think you'll find, though, that this session will flow quite smoothly and effortlessly once the concept is introduced. To help you, here is an idea which you could tailor to your own needs to introduce the metaphor process.

> *In tonight's session we start on the work of Task 2, which is building the company team. Since this is our first step in the process, it might be useful to see how each of us presently views our performance together as a team. To do this we will use an approach called "Insight through Metaphor." The way this works is very simple. What I want you to do is think for a few minutes about the following questions, and then write down in words or draw out in pictures the answers that come to mind. Take your time and develop your thoughts as fully as you can. When everyone is finished, we'll go around the room and share our thoughts. OK? Fine, here are the questions:*

>> *If you were to compare our company's staff or team performance with the characteristics or activities of an animal, plant, machine, or other inanimate object, what would you choose? How does your choice remind you of our team? Take 10 or 15 minutes to think about the questions before writing your answers.*

As a team member yourself, you should do the exercise along with your staff. When finished, go around the room or ask for volunteers, giving each person a chance to share his/her metaphor in great detail. Save your input until last. As the metaphors are shared, capture the central points on the flip chart. After everyone is finished, start a new sheet on which you summarize the ideas presented in the metaphors.

You might wonder why we used a metaphor process instead of the strengths and weaknesses approach that was used in Task 1. The answer is quite simple. By using metaphors and keeping the work focused on team performance, you will end up with a very accurate critique of the current team effort in a way that does not single out any individual staff member (or at least minimizes the possibility of doing so). In short, the staff is looking in the mirror very closely, but not in a way that is likely to be offensive to them.

The length of time necessary to conduct this session can vary greatly. Some groups will get very involved in the spirit of the concept and take the metaphors to great lengths. Other groups may not get that involved. Knowing your staff as you do, you'll probably have a feel for how they will respond to this work. If you think that your staff will make short work of it, you might want to cut this session to an hour, or you might want to go right on into the work of Session 10. Again, whichever approach seems right to you is the one you should take.

Best Image Printing—Metaphors

Customer Service Rep A's Metaphor

The Company Team as a Flowering Plant

Leaves
Stem   *Each of the parts of a plant have a job to do*
Roots   *to produce a flower, fruit or seed*

Air
Pollen   *These ingredients come in like supplies to*
Water   *product*

To this customer service rep, the company team is like a flowering plant with the different staff members comparable to the various parts of the plant. And just as a plant takes in various elements and nutrients to make a flower, fruit or seed, she saw the various team members using the various supplies coming into the business (such as paper and ink) to turn out the company's products. Continuing her metaphor, this staff member went on to explain that just like the various parts of the plant, the company team members had different and specialized functions and tasks, but none could be thought of as being any more important than another.

Typesetter's Metaphor

The Company Team as Migrating Birds

All heading in the same direction
Encounter storms or conflicts, but keep flying
Like a flock of geese heading south
Group heading towards the same goal

The image of the company team as a flock of migrating geese is a powerful one. To this person, the primary team characteristic of her metaphor was that of a group of individuals all heading towards the same goal, and despite difficulties or conflicts encountered in the journey, the members of the team just keep going along together, like geese in a snowstorm, without losing their sense of direction.

Press Operator A's Metaphor

The Company Team as a Printing Press

Requires scheduling
Gather materials and order stock
Requires setting up, just like you have to get ready to run
*   or paste-up*
Requires positioning, just like having the proper stock and
*   the right water balance*
Just as you are ready to run, you discover problems

*When you're running, you try to keep up quality and
    production
Then piles up in delivery
Subject to both external and internal problems*

For this person, the company team was just like a smoothly
(or not so smoothly) running printing press—many
different, separate parts and processes, yet all
interdependent and functioning as a unit. With careful
scheduling, combining of materials, attention to details,
and balancing of processes, potential problems could be
circumvented and the work accomplished. This concept
of the whole organization being represented in his own
machine offered particular insight for this individual and
the other staff as to the importance for balance and
coordinated action if a team is to produce quality results.

Bindery Person's Metaphor

The Company Team as a Giant Earthworm

*Raw material is taken in through the front end of the
    worm, like in the front of the shop
Then the raw materials are transformed, as in typesetting
Next, the transformed materials are processed in the
    colon, like in printing
Finally, the processing is over and the products are pooped
    out, just like in bindery!*

No doubt about it, this metaphor offers a strong image,
and she explained it to the other staff with great enthusiasm!
As she got close to her own particular function in the giant
worm, the staff—who had been totally enchanted with
the image—saw what was coming, and before she could
finish, burst out laughing! Now as we all know, bindery is
not generally thought of as the prestige part of the
printing operation, but through this incredible image, in
less than a minute's time, this woman was able to put the
importance of her function into perspective and endear
herself to the rest of the team in a way that no amount of
lecturing on the importance of team work could have ever
accomplished!

Customer Service Rep B's Metaphor

The Company Team as Spees
(combination of Spiders and Bees)

*Web at front end of shop manned by smiling spider people
Take any bug that comes in the door
Wrap it up – make it into an order!
Pass it back to the beehive for processing*

Come in to my parlor, said the spider to the fly! Perhaps
this image doesn't quite convey the concept of win/win

with respect to customers, but, like the other metaphors, it is very successful in creating the image of specialized sub-teams of individuals working together towards a common goal.

Press Operator B's Metaphor

The Company Team as a Circus

Audience – the customer
Master of Ceremonies – shop owner
Lions – people doing prestige jobs
Elephants – people working on large jobs that move slowly
    but carry a lot of weight
Animals Jumping Obstacles – the team members facing
    and overcoming problems
Fast Cheetahs – people doing jobs requiring fast action,
    like in bindery
Tigers – people doing elegant, quality work
Many Different Acts – lots of different kinds of jobs and
    action, all related, sometimes go on simultaneously

Here is another metaphor creating mental images to which all the staff could relate. To this individual, the metaphor was one of many independent, functioning "acts" which were taking place simultaneously, yet were all part of the "big show," and it offered important team considerations and concepts.

Owner's Metaphor

The Company Team as Bants
(combination of Bees and Ants)

Like bees and ants, all individuals in the shop are in
    constant motion
Also like bees and ants, all individuals are always working,
    but not always accomplishing
When we're working but not accomplishing, we're BANTS

In this metaphor the image of bees and ants buzzing and scurrying around without accomplishing anything illustrates nicely the important concept of teamwork without purpose. The point was well taken. Many teams work very hard, but fail to accomplish anything because they neglect to consider the most important question of all: what is *the right work*?

Session 10
CREATING THE VISION OF YOUR IDEAL COMPANY TEAM—PART A

Goals and Objectives

The goal of this session is for the staff to develop their vision of what the ideal company team should be like.

Specific objectives include:

– allowing each staff member to articulate, share and discuss their team visions with the rest of the staff, and

– introducing basic team concepts to the staff (internal customers, process path, group decision making, and the basic responsibilities of a team member).

Preparatory Information, Learning and Action

In Session 9 we demonstrated the diversity of your staff's perceptions of the company team. Here in Session 10 we will begin the process of developing a *common* vision of what the ideal team for your company could and should be. As facilitator, you will guide your staff through the visioning process, utilizing the same concepts you were introduced to in Chapter 7. First, you will coach your staff to develop their own individual concepts of what the ideal team should be. When this work is complete, you will then begin the task of combining these individual visions into a single vision which can be supported by everyone. It is suggested that at the end of this session you reserve some time to introduce three of the guiding principles which were discussed in Chapter 8 (participative decision making, total quality systems, and internal customers), along with the two new concepts of *process path* and *basic responsibilities of all team members*.

The *process path* is simply the route that a job takes and the various steps it encounters as it passes through your shop from start to finish. Not all jobs will take the same route and not all jobs require the same number of steps. In some cases the process path is simple and direct; in other cases it can be very complicated and may contain repetitive loops. In the case of a job which is susceptible to quality problems or errors, the process path can be exceptionally torturous. In presenting this concept, it might be helpful to draw out the various process paths that you see existing in your shop for various products and services. Figure 12.1 presents the process path at Best Image Printing, which you can use as a model. With these drawings you can easily demonstrate to your staff how the internal customer can change from one job to the next, and how flexibility in team responsibilities and

Figure 12.1

accountabilities can result in a smoother running and more productive and quality-conscious organization.

Depending on the results of your staff's work in this session, it may be appropriate at the end of this session for you to assume your teaching role and spend some time discussing the *basic responsibilities of all team members*. Self-managing teams are a great concept and can yield incredible results; however, they are only effective to the degree that *every* team member assumes personal responsibility in two important ways. First, each team member must assume responsibility and accountability *for their own individual work*. As was mentioned previously, for some workers this can be a difficult transition. Many workers have never experienced a work situation where they

Figure 12.2

THE COLLECTIVE RESPONSIBILITIES FOR
MEMBERS OF A HIGH-PERFORMANCE TEAM

- Each team member has a good understanding of every other team member's individual role and function, and will at all times try to help that person be successful in their role, even if it only involves being sensitive to the problems that person may being experiencing at the time.

- Each team member understands the importance of constant communication and feedback, and is aware that to be effective, communication must move freely and openly in all directions.

- Each team member understands the value of being willing at all times to share knowledge, skills and ideas.

- Each team member strives to create a work environment were team members feel comfortable at all times in sharing their individual thoughts and feelings when discussing or disagreeing on an issue.

---

were not supervised and checked every step of the way. We will discuss your role in this transition more in Phase IV. At this point it is only necessary for you to acknowledge this responsibility and that you will be working with them during the coming weeks to help them assume that responsibility.

The second basic responsibility of every team member is assuming responsibility for the *collective work* or *the total team effort*. The important concept here is that in a true team, there is no such thing as "her problem or his problem." Instead, every problem is shared by all. Certainly a press operator is at the center of the storm when his press goes down; however, all team members should understand that they are also involved in that challenge of solving his problem, and they, too, have an important role to play. In explaining this concept to your staff. You will probably find figure 12.2 useful.

It is highly likely that your staff will hit on many of the team responsibilities listed here in their work in this session. If so, a formal presentation of these ideas may not be necessary, and all you will need to do is coordinate their thoughts and ideas into a unified framework similar to the one above. Suggestions on the best way of introducing this material will be considered in the section on recommendations for implementation.

Case Study and Analysis

The most striking observation that comes from an analysis of the Best Image staff's visions on the ideal team is the *diversity* of understanding about

---

what constitutes a team. Several people confused or combined team characteristics with work flow through the shop (the process path). Some members perceived the value of sharing responsibilities and keeping up communication, whereas others saw value in maintaining effective and efficient compartments where everybody has the responsibility of doing their job perfectly with very little, if any, communication with other departments.

The diversity of response here is probably typical of what any owner might expect when starting on a team building process. One of the reasons for allowing the staff the opportunity to articulate their own vision on the ideal team is to give the owner an idea of the level of understanding that the staff has. Once this is known, it is much easier to provide *appropriate* knowledge and understanding, which you will do at the end of this session. With this understanding, the staff can then undertake the work of Session 11, developing a common vision of the ideal team.

Recommendations for Implementation

It is suggested that you begin this session by introducing the goals and objectives. Once the staff is clear on the purpose of the meeting, you can continue by asking each person to write down their own statement as to what the ideal company team would be like. When they have finished writing, let them share their vision with everyone in as much detail as possible, while you write it on the flip chart. After this sharing is completed, you can point out the common areas, grouping ideas and concepts as much as possible.

When you have finished this synthesis, you will know on which of the concepts (process path, internal customers, total quality, participative decision making, basic responsibilities of team members) you will need to spend the most time. As you introduce these concepts, try to reference and put into context the work that they have just completed. This is also a good time to introduce team concepts which you feel they have overlooked. Remember to finish the session with a brief introduction to Session 11, and explain how in that session they will complete the more difficult task of combining these individual visions into a single vision for the ideal team.

Individual Staff Visions for the Ideal Best Image Printing Team

Customer Service Rep A's Team Vision

1. *Each area does its job to the best of its ability*

2. *The flow of communication is maintained through all departments*

3. *Everyone shares in the responsibility for every customer's job*

Bindery Person's Team Vision

1. Constant flow of information and communication around work in progress

2. Work should be a closed system so that there is no interruption in the process

3. Critical factor is that there is communication in both directions between departments

Press Operator A's Team Vision

1. Front counter – complete invoices, keep track of stock, idea of what job requires in the shop and possible problems, knowledge of limitation of daily production capabilities

2. Typesetter – set type, keep track of proofs, send proofs, proofread

3. Paste-up person – figure out how to design job for press, camera work

4. Bindery – just do bindery, particularly when work load is heavy; have overall knowledge of job as to what is to be done

5. Extra Hand – cut stock, help in bindery, copying, delivery, plate making

6. Boss – overlook operation; does not have to fill in other areas; can keep track of big picture and fill in the communication gaps

Typesetter's Team Vision

Compare the team to a recipe. Intake is brought into the front end. Dry ingredients (typesetting, photocopying, paste-up and camera) are added to liquid ingredients (camera, printing and personnel). These ingredients are mixed together to make the recipe. Some members will then "sample" the recipe as it goes along in the making/ baking process. When all components are mixed together in the right amounts, the product is successful. Depending on the job, some recipes don't require all the ingredients.

Customer Service Rep B's Team Vision

1. Key words are Communicate and Consider

2. *Each person to communicate laterally how on-going factors and changes will affect other's jobs as to the efficiency, time scale, quality and availability*

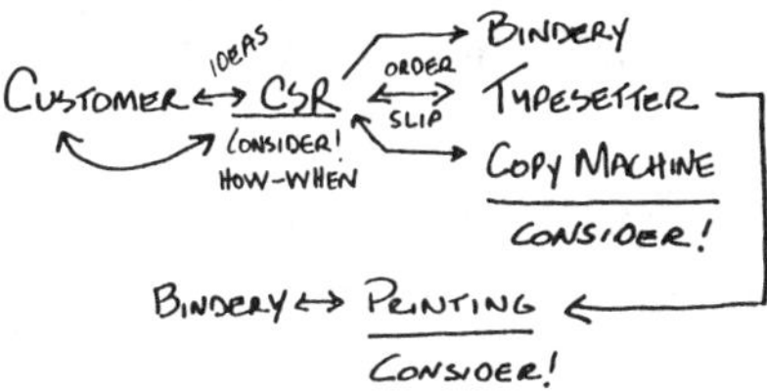

Press Operator B's Team Vision

1. *Work together, but also have camaraderie and harmony*

2. *Communicate well*

3. *Demonstrate good attitudes, positive outlook, and try to minimize negativity*

4. *Have recognizable and achievable goals*

5. *Share knowledge*

6. *Share in solutions to problems*

7. *Have knowledge of one's own area, but can call on other team members*

8. *Work together to minimize stress*

9. *Anticipate problems before they happen and take action*

10. *Know each other's talents and strengths*

11. *Consider everyone responsible*

12. *Ask questions and don't assume*

13. *Are happy with their work*

Session 11
CREATING THE VISION OF YOUR IDEAL COMPANY TEAM—PART B

Goals and Objectives

The goal of this session is for the staff to create a statement articulating the Ten Key Characteristics of the ideal company team.

Specific objectives include:

– having each staff member articulate what they consider to be the ten key characteristics of a team and team member,

Figure 12.3

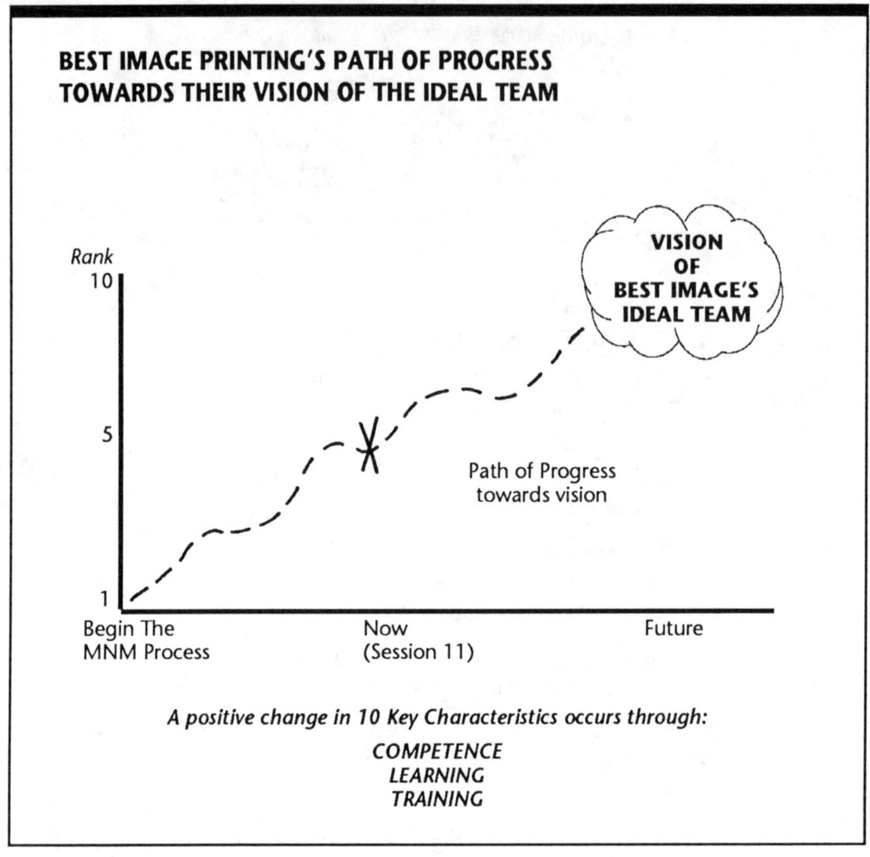

- combining the individual lists into a single statement of team characteristics which has the support of all staff, and

- developing the "now" position or snapshot in time of where the team presently sees itself relative to its ideal vision.

Preparatory Information, Learning and Action

In this session your staff will complete their team visioning work by creating a statement on the Ten Key Characteristics of the Ideal Company Team. This statement is a major accomplishment for your staff as it will become the guiding vision for the team from this time forward. The session will finish with the staff individually comparing the ten characteristics they defined with their perceptions of the present state of team development.

This session introduces two additional concepts: developing group consensus and the Path to the Ideal Vision.

Group consensus, when properly developed, is perhaps the most powerful tool that any owner can employ when striving to reach a desired objective. Sometimes consensus can be easily achieved; more commonly, however, it requires considerable effort and time. As facilitator, it is critical that you maintain a neutral role during the consensus building part of this session.

The Path to the Ideal Vision diagram is shown in figure 12.3 (which is actually a simplified version of figure 2.1). By using this diagram as a model, it is possible to show and monitor progress towards *any* ideal vision, in this case the Ideal Best Image Team.

Case Study Discussion and Analysis

A comparison of the Best Image case study results for Sessions 10 and 11 shows that by the time the staff had completed identifying the ten key characteristics, they had developed significant consensus around the concept of an ideal team. Although the process had been slow, the result was a vision in which all staff members could support and take ownership. Ownership in such work is essential, for as we will see in the next task (that of ranking the degree of current development of each characteristic), all staff members could enthusiastically participate in the process because they were anxious to see where the team was now, relative to *their* desired vision. Had the owner developed the same list of characteristics and asked the staff to rank themselves, the process would not have received this unanimous support.

If you look at the staff averages for the "now" condition of the characteristics, and compare them with the owner's rankings, it can be seen that overall the staff graded their performance more severely than the owner, by about 10%. Although you might not expect it, this is a common result in team self-analysis.

More interesting than the actual rankings, however, is the fact that, with a couple of exceptions, both staff and owner recognized the same weak points and strong points. Because of this agreement, there was no question about which areas needed work. Conversely, both saw cooperation as a strong point.

The area of greatest discrepancy was that of consistency. Because the staff saw the Ten Key Characteristics as *their* work, they were very interested in finding out *why* the owner ranked consistency as he did and then doing something about it, than they would have been had the owner made a statement about having to work on consistency. Again, the power of staff ownership and consensus in effecting positive change within an organization cannot be overemphasized.

Recommendations for Implementation

When facilitating this session, it is essential that you maintain a neutral and non-attached position with respect to your staff's work. Remember, *it is their work,* and what seems so simple, obvious and desirable to you in terms of team characteristics, may not be for them. Let them develop their own vision for their team. After all, although you are a team member, too, they are setting the standards for their own behavior and performance during the months to come.

The Path to the Ideal Vision diagram is one which you will refer to again in later sessions and is discussed in detail as Resource Tool C in The MNM Tool Box. You may want to refer to Resource Tool C and make a copy of the generic version of the diagram to give to your staff as you explain the concept. Then, as you move into the task of comparing the Ten Key Characteristics with your "now" position, you can draw your own version of the diagram on the flip chart to show how their immediate task relates to the general concept.

In concluding this session you should introduce the work of the next two sessions—developing strategic plans for improving the team deficiencies as were identified in this session. It is quite likely that your staff will feel empowered by the work they have done here, and you should take time to acknowledge and commend them for this good work.

Creating the Vision of the Ideal Best Image Team

Task: Identify 5-10 key characteristics, traits, attributes of the <u>ideal</u> future Best Image team member/team. Here are the traits suggested.

Best Image Staff Listing of Key Team Characteristics

Person A	Person B	Person C	Person D	Person E	Person F
Consistency	Flexible	Organized	Talent	Communicative	Grace under
Flexibility	Integrity	Communicative	Skill	Responsible	pressure
Professionalism	Cooperative	Efficient	Experienced	Fast paced	Patience
Competence	Communicative	Courteous	Communicative	Knowledge of	Perception of
Overall know-	Tolerant	Considerate	Quality con-	other areas	the whole
edge and	Efficient	Detail oriented	scious	Knowledge of	Orderliness
understanding	Considerate	Pressure sensitive	Attentiveness	weaknesses	Empathy
	Positive		No assumption		Effective com-
			Efficient (getting		munication
			job done as		
			quickly as possible)		
			Pride in finished work		

Of the 20 different traits listed above, the next task was to list the 10 most important ones. It was decided not to rate them, as each is equally important. Following is the group's consensus of the ideal traits:

Ten Key Characteristics of the
Ideal Best Image Printing Team and Team Member

Communicative
Responsible
Skilled/Experienced
Efficient/Organized
Quality Conscious/Integrity/Pride
Cooperative
Flexible
Considerate/Tolerant/Patient
Positive/Pressure Sensitive
Consistent

Here the concept of the Path to the Ideal Vision was introduced, along with how the 10 key characteristics could be used as a standard for measuring future improvements in team performance. Then the characteristics were individually ranked in terms of now vs. ideal.

Task: *Establish the "now" position by ranking the 10 characteristics as you see them exhibited by the group, using the following scale:*

$$1 - 2 - 3 - 4 - 5 - 6 - 7 - 8 - 9 - 10$$

Poorly	Adequate	Well
Developed		Developed
or Terrible		or Exceptional

Characteristic	Staff Rankings	Group Average	Owner's Ranking	
Communicative	6,6,8,5,7,8	6.7	8	
Responsible	7,6,8,9,7,7	7.3	8	
Skilled	6,5,7,2,7,7	5.7	5	Needs work
Efficient	6,5,7,1,6,7	5.3	5	Needs work
Quality	8,6,7,6,5,8	6.7	7	
Cooperative	6,7,8,7,8,9	7.5	10	Highest
Flexible	6,6,7,8,8,7	7.0	8	
Considerate	6,7,8,5,7,8	6.8	10	
Positive	6,6,7,5,8,7	6.5	8	
Consistent	7,5,7,8,7,8	7.0	5	Needs work
	Averages	6.7	7.4	

Session 12
INITIATING THE TEAM IMPROVEMENT PROCESS—PART A

Goals and Objectives

The goal of this session and the next two sessions is to initiate a team improvement process focusing on the weakest of the Ten Key Characteristics, as identified in the last session.

Specific objectives for the staff include:

- brainstorming to identify primary sources of deficiencies,
- brainstorming to identify potential strategic action which could correct team weaknesses, and
- brainstorming to identify potential monitoring systems to evaluate the progress in team improvement.

Preparatory Information, Learning and Action

Sessions 12 through 14 can be considered transitional sessions in The MNM Process. Some of the work is clearly Phase III work in that it focuses on existing company systems; yet, some of the work involves actual implementation of ideas for improvement, which is the primary work of Phase IV (see figure 2.1). This transitional aspect will become clear as you read through these sessions and into the next chapter.

The Path to the Ideal Vision concept presented in Resource Tool C can be used to move your company from its existing situation ("now" position) to achieve any desired ideal vision. You and your staff will use this concept extensively throughout the rest of The MNM Process, so it is important that you review and understand Resource Tool C thoroughly before facilitating this session.

In the last session we established the "now" position of your company's Ten Key Characteristics relative to its ideal team vision (see figure 12.3). Here in Session 12, and again in the next two sessions, we will initiate an improvement process aimed at moving the perceived team weaknesses from the "now" position along the Path of Progress to the ideal vision. Each of these three sessions will utilize staff participation to:

- identify possible sources for the perceived weakness or problem,
- identify potential strategic action for correcting the problem, and
- identify potential systems for monitoring the effectiveness of the improvement process.

As we discussed in Session 1, some of the ideas which come from these sessions you will want to implement immediately; some you will introduce on a short-term basis, say, several weeks; and some will require long-term action extending over several months.

From this point on in The MNM Process it is important that *action on all suggested ideas be taken as soon as appropriate.* Since this session begins the implementation of the on-going improvement work of Phase IV, it is appropriate that action on any immediate and short-term ideas be taken as soon as possible. Implementation of some of the ideas will be entirely your responsibility as shop owner, while others can be delegated entirely to your staff. And there will be ideas that can be implemented by you and your staff together. Action on ideas which are more long-term in nature can be postponed until Phase V.

Case Study Discussion and Analysis

The most important aspect of this session was that it demonstrated quite clearly to the Best Image staff how The MNM Process could be used to improve and achieve *any* aspect of the company's vision. It also demonstrated the effectiveness of group problem solving and how group brainstorming could generate, within a very short time, a wealth of potential solutions for complex problems. Certainly this session did not exhaust all of the possible ideas for improving consistency in product quality and customer service, but it did initiate the on-going process of improvement and identify methods for evaluating the progress being made.

In this session Best Image's staff and owner were able to develop numerous ideas for improving the consistency in product quality and customer service. Many of the ideas could be immediately implemented, while some would require joint action over a longer period of time. The session closed by dividing up the tasks to be done, and with the understanding that everyone would make a strong effort during the next two weeks to implement those ideas which fell into the immediate category.

Recommendations for Implementation

You should begin this session with an overview of the material presented in the Path to the Ideal Vision (Resource Tool C). For this presentation you may want to prepare your own version of figure 12.3, illustrating your "now" position with respect to the ideal team, based on your work in Session 11.

After you are sure that your staff fully understands the purpose of this session, you should allow them to select which of the Ten Key Characteristics they would like to examine first. It really doesn't make any difference which of the deficient characteristics you begin with, as the primary objective of this session is to demonstrate *the process*. Also, it is probably not good to spend too much time in raising expectations that this first session will yield exceptional results. Although many of the suggestions may indeed be extremely useful, it is far better to reinforce to your staff that this process becomes more productive the more it is used.

Best Image Team Improvement Process

During the last session everyone ranked the "now" position of the 10 Key Characteristics of the Ideal Best Image Team on a scale of 1-10 (1=poorly developed; 10=well developed). In looking at the rankings for "consistent," there is a difference of 2 between how the group sees themselves and how the owner sees the group. In discussing the reasons for the ranking, the owner said that he perceived a lack of consistency primarily in two areas: product quality and customer service. It was decided that these two areas would be considered separately.

PRODUCT QUALITY

Possible Reasons for Lack of Consistency

1. Too much work at one time

2. Too little work at one time

3. Doing too many things at one time

The key to solving this problem is in <u>staying aware</u>. Be aware that during these times you may not pay enough attention to product quality.

Strategic Plan for Improving Consistency

1. Ensure that invoices are properly filled out
   a. Complete training of customer service rep B on counter
   b. BE AWARE
   d. Check paper requirements
   d. Be systematic
   e. Have bin for incomplete invoices

2. Ensure that paper is trimmed consistently
   a. Uniform procedure on cutter (press operators and bindery person will work out)

3. Cross training in quality defects

4. Develop system for identifying quality problems as to probable cause; keep a log

Immediate Implementation: 1b, 1c, 1d, 1e, 2a, 4
Short-term Implementation: 1a,
Long-term Implementation: 3

How to Monitor Progress of Improvement Plan

1. Correctly completed invoices improve product quality;
   how to monitor:
   a. less backlog
   b. higher monthly sales volume because of fewer
      errors and reworks
   c. use blue paper invoice for reprints, marked with
      reason for rework
   d. use yellow highlighter on white copy of invoice to
      note areas of missing information (tabulate on
      weekly basis)

2. Uniform operator procedure on cutter could be
   monitored by
   a. Including as part of a periodic cross-training skills
      review

3. Cross-training in quality defects could be monitored by
   a. Including as part of a periodic cross-training skills
      review and update

4. Type and cause of quality problems could be monitored by
   a. Having an external customer complaint form which
      is tabulated weekly
   b. Having an internal customer error/complaint form
      which is tabulated weekly

CUSTOMER SERVICE

Possible Reasons for Lack of Consistency

1. Conditions at front counter are constantly changing —
   number of customers waiting, number of staff available, phones ringing

2. Space at front counter is limited

3. Children are distraction to parents

4. Variation in turn-around times due to number of orders
   in shop, staff on vacation or sick, failure to return
   proofs on time, failure to order paper

Strategic Plan for Improving Consistency

1. For dealing with customers at the counter:
   a. Back up co-workers to greater extent; ask for help
   b. Stay alert to what's going on in the front —
      EVERYONE
   c. Acknowledge customer's presence even if you can't
      help them immediately

      d. *Immediately tend to customers who just have a quick question, or wish to drop something off*
      e. *Have a task force to evaluate utilization of front space*
      f. *Have crayons and paper available for children*

2. *For dealing with varying turn-around times:*
      a. *Let customer know that they are getting something really fast because ... (tell them the reason)*
      b. *Let customers know if there is a backlog*
      c. *Let customers know when people are on vacation (which typically creates a backlog)*
      d. *Emphasize importance of return of proofs by a certain date*
      e. *Develop a "tips for proofing" hand out sheet which includes turn-around data*
      f. *Develop a post-it note to go on proofs*
      g. *Get an alarm clock to remind about ordering paper*

Immediate Implementation: 1a-d, 1f, 2a-d
Short-term Implementation: 1e, 2e-g

How to Monitor Progress of Ways to Improve Consistency

1. *Customer service at counter could be monitored by:*
      a. *Owner periodically observing and reporting to staff*
      b. *Post a reminder behind counter for everyone to look at on a regular basis (like a "wash your hands before returning to work" sign)*
      c. *Have a "counter irregularities" form which is tabulated weekly*

2. *Consistency in turn-around times could be monitored by:*
      a. *Have complaint form which is tabulated weekly*
      b. *Have press operators tabulate number of times they couldn't run because of proof not being returned*

Session 13
INITIATING THE TEAM IMPROVEMENT PROCESS—PART B

Goals and Objectives

The goal of this session is to continue the team improvement process begun in the last session by focusing on additional weakness identified in the Ten Key Characteristics.

Specific objectives for this session are the same as for the last session and include:

  – brainstorming to identify primary sources of deficiencies,

- brainstorming to identify potential strategic action which could correct team weaknesses, and

- brainstorming to identify potential monitoring systems to evaluate the progress in team improvement.

Preparatory Information, Learning and Action

It is important that implementation of the ideas designated for immediate action in Session 12 be started prior to conducting this session. This will ensure the continued enthusiastic participation of the staff.

Staff training and education are a critical component of every company team. Since it is highly likely that you will focus on this area at some point, The Learning Curve Continuum has been included as Resource Tool D. You should find it a useful source of ideas and concepts for evaluating the current skill and learning levels of your staff and developing a plan for systematic improvement.

In this session, Best Image focused on improving skill and learning levels among their team members and reference is made to the central concepts presented in the Learning Curve Continuum. Since many of the skill and learning issues which Best Image faces are similar to those which you may encounter in your improvement process, it is useful to consider the Learning Curve Continuum before proceeding.

The Learning Curve Continuum is a useful concept for describing the fundamental levels of competency that a person might have in any skill or area of knowledge. As shown in figure 12.4, this curve recognizes five basic levels:

Mastery
Proficiency
Competency
Understanding
Awareness

General working definitions for each of these levels are presented in Resource Tool D. These working definitions can be modified for specific job functions and skills to develop an objective scale for evaluating an individual's or team's progress along the Learning Curve. In Phase IV we will look at several ways in which the Learning Curve Continuum can be applied.

Case Study Discussion and Analysis

During Session 11 Best Image identified their skills as an area that needed improvement. Many times quality and productivity suffer greatly because a worker does not have adequate training or understanding about a certain

Figure 12.4

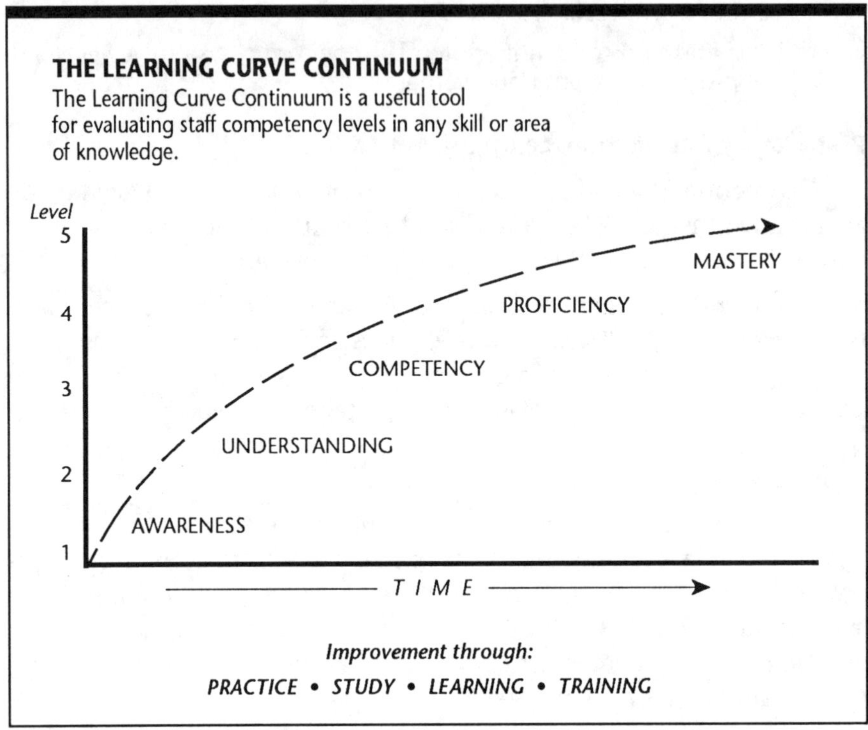

task or machine and feels uncomfortable in saying anything about it. Staff sessions such as this one can be extremely valuable in that they show workers that *everyone* has areas where they could use some more training, and that not only is it all right to express a need for more training, but it is actually encouraged.

By introducing the Learning Curve Continuum *after* the staff had expressed their need for additional skill training and learning, they were able to immediately see its practical application. In addition, they were able to see that it provided an *objective* method for looking at personal deficiencies in a non-threatening manner which could lead to long-term improvement and greater job satisfaction.

Recommendations for Implementation

Regardless of what topic your staff decides to introduce in this session, you might still want to consider introducing the Learning Curve Continuum as its concepts are applicable to any skill or area of knowledge that might need improvement.

Again, regardless of which topic you consider in this session, it is important to take the time to categorize strategic ideas in terms of immediate, short-term and long-term action, and then begin the implementation process. Perhaps nothing will have as great a positive *or negative* effect on the outcome of The MNM Process from this point forward as your diligence in doing those things you said you would.

Best Image Printing Individual Learning Needs

Each staff member was asked to list areas, skills and knowledge in which they felt they needed or wanted more training or a better understanding. Each individual then presented his/her perceived needs to the rest of the staff.

Perceived Learning Needs of Customer Service Rep A:

- *More product knowledge, i.e. specific papers*
- *Knowledge of camera work*
- *How to deal with irate customers on the phone*
- *Attention to details, such as invoices*
- *More knowledge of pricing, specifically typesetting*
- *More effective time management*
- *Better understanding of quality aspects of high-speed copiers*

Perceived Learning Needs of Press Operator A:

- *More knowledge on color*
- *Develop greater patience with other staff members when being asked questions*
- *Better understanding of 2nd color unit*

Perceived Learning Needs of Bindery Person:

- *Better understanding of folder, some stocks are more difficult than others*
- *Better understanding of which jobs are priority*
- *Knowledge of other team members' jobs*

Perceived Learning Needs of Press Operator B:

- *Better understanding of the process path*
- *Better understanding of press adjustments, particularly up and down; imaging*
- *Become quicker at anticipating quality problems*
- *Learning to control temper*
- *Become more attentive; learn to think faster about jobs*
- *Learn to perf and score faster*
- *Need to produce more*

Perceived Learning Needs of Typesetter:

- *Become better at proofing, particularly spelling*
- *Become more proficient at using drawing software*
- *Become better at stripping negatives*

- *Learn better time management, i.e. not to stop working on project to take care of walk-ins*
- *Pay closer attention to the way invoices are written, particularly for special paper requirements*

Perceived Learning Needs of Customer Service Rep B:

- *Become better at time management, i.e. losing track of copying projects when phone rings*
- *Need to understand pricing better*
- *Become more skillful and efficient in dealing with customers, other staff members, and shop owner, all at same time*
- *Need to know more about high-speed copiers in terms of adjusting quality and routine maintenance*

At this point the Learning Curve Continuum was introduced and some time was spent in applying it to the above lists of perceived learning needs, and discussing how it could be used to monitor improvement of specific skills and job functions through time.

Potential Strategic Action for Improving Individual and Team Learning

1. *Team members should share learning and skills with others on the team*

2. *Need to make a comprehensive study of skill and learning needs of each individual and implement a skill and learning improvement program*
   a. *Each individual should make a list of skills and knowledge required for each of their roles and functions and rank themselves using the Learning Curve Continuum scale*
   b. *Shop owner should make a second list of skills and knowledge for each of the staff roles and rank each of them using the Learning Curve Continuum*
   c. *Combine results of 2a and 2b to get training/ learning needs assessment*
   d. *Implement on-going program of skill and learning improvement*

3. *Investigate sources of skill and learning aids*
   a. *Audio and video tapes*
   b. *Check out printing and computer design courses in area*
   c. *Check out appropriate general business skills courses at local colleges and universities*
   d. *Investigate possibility of getting a tour of related industry facilities: i.e. paper mill, ink manufacturer*

Immediate Implementation: 3a-d
Short-term Implementation: 1, 2a-c, 3d
Long-term Implementation: 1, 2d

> **Potential Monitoring Systems to Evaluate Progress in Improving Skills and Learning**
>
> 1. Cross-training and sharing of skills and learning could be monitored by:
>   a. Shop owner periodically observing and reporting to staff
>   b. Conducting a Learning Curve Continuum Assessment on a periodic basis
>
> 2. Implement a skill and learning improvement program
>   a. Utilize Learning Curve Continuum Assessment every six months

Session 14
INITIATING THE TEAM IMPROVEMENT PROCESS—PART C

Goals and Objectives

The goal of this session is to continue the team improvement process begun in the last two sessions by focusing on additional weaknesses identified in the Ten Key Characteristics.

Specific objectives for this session are also the same as for the last two sessions and include:

- brainstorming to identify primary sources of deficiencies,

- brainstorming to identify potential strategic action which could correct team weaknesses, and

- brainstorming to identify potential monitoring systems to evaluate the progress in team improvement.

Preparatory Information, Learning and Action

In this session you should continue to focus on those areas of your Ten Key Characteristics that need improvement. Although this session is the last session in the book devoted to exploring team deficiencies, you shouldn't discontinue the team building sessions simply to move on to Phase IV. If you still have areas of the Ten Key Characteristics which need immediate improvement, by all means continue the sessions until you have explored each one. Again, you should consider The MNM Team Building Process as a model, not as a template. The MNM Process is designed to be a flexible process that each company can tailor to its own needs. So utilize the concepts and sessions presented in this book as you and your staff find them appropriate.

Mindstorming, a concept presented in Resource Tool E, is another useful approach to problem solving. Mindstorming (sometimes referred to as mind

Figure 12.5 ■ From Best Image Printing Session 14

**MINDSTORMING RESULTS OF EXPLORING
WAYS TO IMPROVE EFFICIENCY**

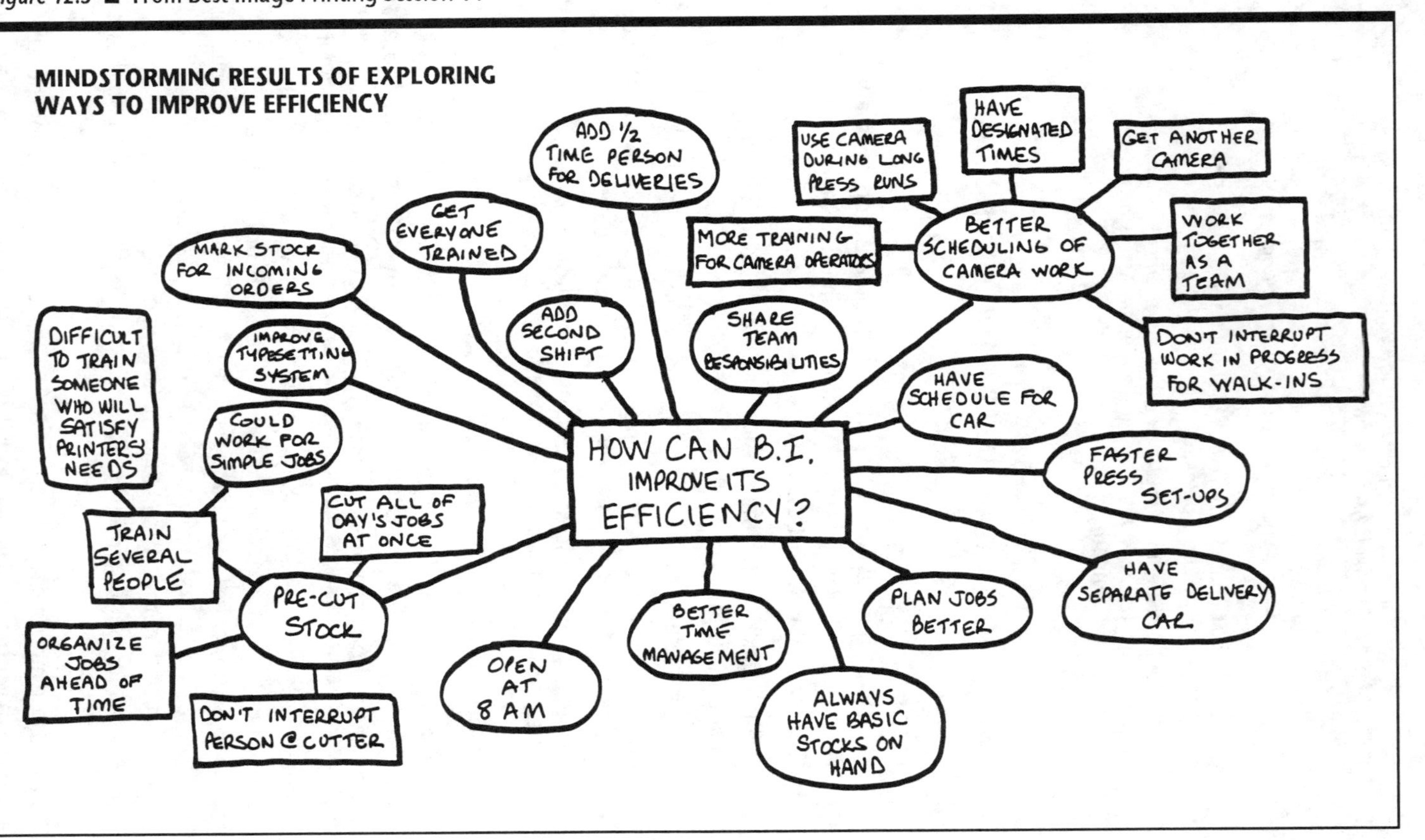

Figure 12.6 ■ From Best Image Printing Session 14

MINDSTORMING RESULTS IN OUTLINE FORM

This is the same information that's presented in the mindstorming diagram above. Here it is written in outline form and includes some additional comments that were made but not put on the diagram.

HOW CAN BEST IMAGE IMPROVE ITS EFFICIENCY

1. Add second shift
2. Plan jobs better
3. Open at 8 AM instead of 8:30
4. Have schedule for car
   - pick up and delivery doesn't mean we're a courier service
   - pick up time will influence ultimate delivery date
5. Have separate car for deliveries
6. Make sure basic papers are always on hand
7. Mark stock for incoming orders
8. Faster press setups
9. Share team responsibilities
   - split work where appropriate
10. Improve typesetting system
11. Have precut stock
    a. train several people
       - difficult to train someone who will satisfy printers' needs
       - could work for simpler jobs
    b. cut all day's jobs at one time
    c. organize jobs ahead of time
    d. person cutting stock cannot be interrupted
12. Better time management
13. Get everyone fully trained
14. Add part-time person for deliveries
15. Better scheduling of camera work
    a. More training for camera operators
       - customer service rep A is being trained and customer service rep B will be trained next month
       - when training is in progress, it is essential that other activities be covered by a team member; the person learning the camera cannot be expected to also work at the counter and answer the phones!
    b. have designated times for camera work
       - do camera work at 12 noon every day; work that comes in before noon can be done that day, while work coming in after noon will be done the next day.
       - will require changing lunch schedules
       - have a definite system for covering the counter and doing the camera work
    c. get another camera
    d. use camera during long runs
    e. don't disrupt work in progress for walk-ins
    f. more training for camera operators

mapping) contains elements of the futuring process we saw earlier in Strategic Futuring (Resource Tool B), and is quite similar to the brainstorming process we used extensively in earlier sessions. The primary difference between Mindstorming and ordinary brainstorming is in the way the information is presented. Unlike the brainstorming process, where ideas are *listed* in the order that people think of them and *without showing any particular relationships between the ideas*, the Mindstorming process *actually maps out the interrelationships of ideas as they are generated.*

Using Mindstorming is quite simple. Starting from a central idea or question which is circled on a flip chart, thoughts and ideas are solicited from the group and added to the sheet with lines showing linkage to other thoughts already expressed on the board. As in the standard brainstorming process, judgement is suspended at this idea-generating stage. If necessary, ideas can be judged through consensus later. However, this probably won't be necessary as the truly innovative thoughts will serve as seeds to generate whole new branches of thought and understanding. Ideas which are not as relevant or appropriate will, in a sense, die on the vine and not be considered further.

Mindstorming is an excellent team building technique and encourages the active participation of all present. It is also a very useful tool for individual exploration of ideas and options. As is explained in Resource Tool E, Mindstorming encourages a totally different thinking style than is utilized in simply listing options.

Case Study Discussion and Analysis

In this session Best Image focused on the last of the three greatest perceived weaknesses in their company team—efficiency. To explore this weakness the owner used the Mindstorming concept.

Best Image's Mindstorming diagram (figure 12.5) was generated by the staff in about one hour. Numerous ideas were presented, some of which were truly innovative and would lead to further exploration and insight for improvement. Others served as grist for the mill, to keep the process going and focused. Most important, however, is the fact that because every member's idea was included in the diagram, everyone felt that they had ownership in the whole diagram. Because of this, they will be inclined to participate even more in the future. And in all probability, some of the participants whose ideas fell short in this session will undoubtedly become the shining star in a future meeting. This is what team problem solving and brainstorming is all about—understanding that the product of the group will generally come closer to solving the problem, and that just as in any team sport, every individual will have his/her big day.

It is important to note that those suggestions requiring a large outlay of money (such as "buy another camera" and "buy a car for deliveries") are made long-term goals rather than discarded for being expensive/impractical/impossible. Handling it in this manner reinforces the value of every contribution.

Mindstorming results can be presented in both diagrammatic and outline form. In studying the two Mindstorming formats, do you find that you prefer one over another? Have you figured out why yet? (You'll find the answer in Resource Tool A.)

Improving Team Efficiency

In this session we used the mindstorming technique to discover how we could improve our efficiency. The results are recorded in both diagram and outline forms.

Implementation is as follows (ideas not listed will not be pursued at this time):

Immediate Implementation: 2, 3, 9, 12, 15, 15a, 15d, 15e, 15f

Short-term Implementation: 4, 6, 7, 8, 9, 10, 11a, 11c, 12, 13, 15a

Long-term Implementation: 1, 4, 5, 10, 13, 14, 15c

Summary

The overall goal of Task 2 has been to develop your staff into a highly motivated and proficient self-managing team. Your success in reaching this goal depends on many factors, the most important being the point where your staff began the process. If your staff's experience has included a strong sense of teamwork, then probably six sessions similar to Best Image's will be sufficient in achieving that goal. If you are starting the process with a group of strong "independent operators," you may require twice as many sessions.

The important thing is to keep the team focusing outward on the issues and problems that are still presenting barriers, be they barriers to individuals or barriers to the team. It is critically important for you as facilitator/coach/leader/owner (what a lot of hats!) to continue to give credit were credit is due, particularly *team* credit. And also remember that even though the team (and probably you, yourself) may *think* that they are now *really* productive, the reality is that they have just begun!

The MNM Process is an on-going process based on the belief that there are *always* ways of improving. And that it is this continuing discovery of a better way that makes the team approach to business so rewarding and personally satisfying.

In Phase IV we will explore in detail the concept of on-going improvement. Now that the team has finished warming up and is in shape, we can get down to working on some really serious challenges!

On-Going

Improvement

Work

CHAPTER 13

ON-GOING IMPROVEMENT WORK

The overall goal of Phase IV is to develop and implement a continuous and on-going system for improvement which builds upon and utilizes the concepts and understanding developed in Phase III. With completion of the analytical phase of your company's "now" position relative to your overall ideal vision, the focus of The MNM Team Building Process becomes totally pro-active, with each session designed to move your company further along the Path of Progress towards its envisioned goals.

As you can see in figure 2.1, it is at this point in the process that significant increases in productivity and improvement in quality should start to emerge. Again, as changes are implemented, you can expect to experience some plateaus and dips in the Path of Progress; these fluctuations are expected and should be temporary.

We begin Phase IV by presenting two additional sessions as models for guiding the on-going improvement work. Both of these sessions will utilize a format similar to that used in Phase III. Session 15 will focus on *developing a system* for the improvement work of future sessions, and Session 16 will offer suggestions for *implementing this system*. Each of these sessions will continue the case study of Best Image Printing and offer possible ideas and suggestions for your own implementation.

Session 15
DEVELOPING A SYSTEM FOR CONTINUOUS, ON-GOING IMPROVEMENT

Goals and Objectives

The goal of this session is to develop a system which will guide the continuous and on-going improvement of your company in the months and years ahead.

Specific objectives will be to:

- develop a format and agenda for the Phase IV improvement meetings,
- develop monitoring systems to guide the process, and
- establish priorities for implementing the short-term action plans developed in Phase III.

Preparatory Information, Learning and Action

The Phase IV improvement meetings differ from the Phase III meetings in that they are *action* oriented as opposed to *learning and understanding* oriented. Actually, the work of Phase IV began in the last three sessions of Task 2, when the staff began considering ways of correcting the weaknesses they saw in the Ten Key Characteristics. Here in Session 15 we will formalize this improvement process by using input from the staff to develop the format and agenda for subsequent meetings.

It is important to mention that the work of Phase IV will focus on the company as a whole, as well as on the development of the self-managing team. From this point onward in The MNM Process it is suggested that the frequency of your meetings be cut back to every three weeks, with the option of every two weeks when necessary. The reason for suggesting this is that in Phase IV there are many areas of related work that will be going on simultaneously—implementation of Phase IV strategic action, special project work by staff, and the work which you will be doing as owner in Phase V. You should discuss the frequency of meetings with your staff at the beginning of this session, but experience has shown that with the additional work everyone will have, every three weeks is about right. If you go to four weeks, there is a chance that the improvement work will lose momentum and get lost in the shuffle.

As in the Phase III work, it is important that an agenda be distributed prior to meetings and that input be solicited from the staff ahead of time to be put on the agenda. Minutes should be prepared detailing the meeting and handed out for staff to put in their MNM Process binders. Again, diligence in providing the minutes in a regular and timely manner will contribute greatly to the success of the process and provide a written record of what's been discussed.

Another change you might want to consider in the meeting format at this point is the option of giving other staff members a chance at facilitating the improvement meetings on a rotating basis. The advantages of this option are that it would develop greater responsibility and accountability in the staff and would stimulate renewed interest in the meetings. The only disadvantage would be if you thought that in doing so you would be giving up too much control.

At the beginning of this session you should reintroduce the Path to the Ideal Vision which was discussed in Sessions 11 and 12 and which is detailed in Resource Tool C. By doing this you can demonstrate how this concept can be used as a model for continuous on-going improvement for *any* aspect of your company.

You might want to introduce in this session the concept that by implementing the Phase IV Improvement Process, your company is implementing a form of preventive maintenance. Many people are firm believers in "if it ain't broke, don't fix it." Yet just as replacing a worn tire or bearing in your car *before it goes* can save you big headaches and repair bills, so can the Phase IV improvement work serve to identify problems still in the formative stage before they explode into issues requiring crisis management. Today more and more companies accept preventive maintenance as an integral part of a total quality system. When considered in this sense, the return on investment for involvement in the Phase IV process goes far beyond increased productivity and improved quality.

The final objective for this session will be to take the opportunities and potential short-term strategic action plans identified in Sessions 1 through 14 (and possibly some of the strategic plans that you developed in Chapter 9) and rank them in terms of priority of implementation. You will need to go back through the minutes of each of Sessions 1-14 and through your own strategic visioning work of Chapter 9 and compile a list of identified short-term opportunities and strategies, as well as any immediate opportunities or strategic action plans which have not yet been implemented. Then, depending on your personal management style, you have the option of doing some advance prioritizing on your own or letting the team do the work in Session 15.

Case Study Discussion and Analysis

Not only did the work done in this session provide Best Image with a comprehensive action plan to guide their improvement work over the next several months, it was also effective in providing the team with a good collective overview and understanding, in a very practical way, of the purpose and potential value of the next phase of The MNM Process. Finally, since the staff had participated in identifying and prioritizing the work to be done, there would be no problem in getting their commitment, both as individuals and as a team, to the programs.

Recommendations for Implementation

It is quite possible, due to the amount of material, for this session to take more than one meeting. The preparatory work that you do prior to this meeting, particularly the assembly and categorizing of the short-term opportunities and potential strategic action plans, will greatly facilitate the work of this session.

This session will set the tone for all of the Phase IV work to come. It is important, therefore, that you devote as much time as needed to it to ensure that your goals and objectives are accomplished. Much of the work will be review of concepts already introduced or ideas and strategic action plans conceived in earlier sessions, so the session should not be difficult to facilitate or understand.

Best Image Printing
Developing a Format for On-Going Improvement

The team reviewed their progress to date by looking at their current position on their path to the ideal vision.

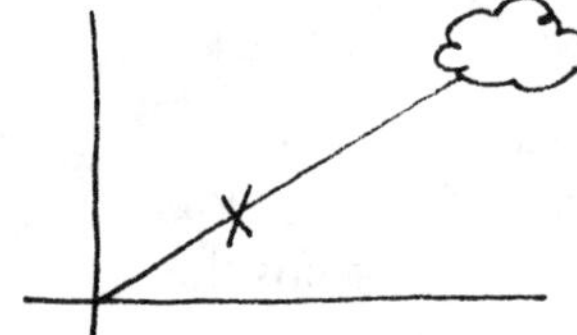

Following this, the meeting focused on developing a format by which the team could monitor its progress during the next phase, and ensure continuing progress and improvement.

It was decided that periodic meetings would work well, with the following agenda being standard.

Agenda for Future Meetings

1. Review issues from previous meeting
*   a. action taken and progress made*
*   b. problems experienced*

2. Current position
*   a. Sales report*
*   b. General market conditions*
*   c. Customers—new, old, lost*

3. Problem identification and group problem solving
*   a. Identify significant or chronic problem, such as*
*   1. reprints and rework*
*   2. schedules and deadlines*
*   3. equipment*
*   4. customer service*

    b. Group problem solving
       1. brainstorming/mindstorming for possible solutions
       2. delegation of staff to pursue promising options
    c. Devise new approaches/systems

4. Internal operations, such as
    a. team and staff issues
    b. communication
    c. ordering of supplies
    d. scheduling

5. Quality issues

6. Other areas of concern, such as
    a. special jobs coming up
    b. personnel issues—vacations or time off
    c. equipment down

7. Successes

8. Other

Future Meeting Format

1. Participatory meeting with agenda to focus/prompt discussion

2. Rotating facilitator option

3. Agenda will be prepared two days in advance of meeting

4. Owner will prepare agenda from items given to him by staff

5. Minutes will be taken at each meeting and distributed afterwards. These will be reviewed at the next meeting.

As issues/problems/questions/items for discussion arise, team members are encouraged to jot them down and give to owner so that they can be included in the minutes and not forgotten.

Meetings will be held every three weeks. The option remains open to have meetings every two weeks if needed.

All of the above can be modified at any time with the approval of the group, in order to meet the needs of the group.

The last item focused on prioritizing the opportunities developed in Sessions 1-14. Following is the group's Top 10 Action Plan, in order of priority.

	Vision Component	Action Plan
1	Marketing & Sales	Do total review of marketing program and its effectiveness

	Vision Component	Action Plan
2	Staff Team	Do comprehensive study of skill and learning needs of each individual; implement a skill and learning improvement program
3	Marketing & Sales / Economy	Develop marketing plan focused on recession-proof customers
4	Competition	Install color copier ASAP
5	Competition / Customers	Conduct survey of our customers to determine how we are doing relative to their expectations and experience with competition
6	Products & Services / Customers	Staff to develop written policy concerning deadlines, proofing and typical production schedule
7	Products & Services / Customers	Begin cross-training team
8	Facilities	Improve work environment by reducing noise, improving air quality, and improving lighting
9	Equipment	Staff to develop a preventive maintenance schedule for their equipment, based on manuals and conversations with manufacturers
10	Customers	Staff to develop workshop for educating customers in how to design and produce better mechanicals

Session 16
IMPLEMENTING YOUR SYSTEM OF CONTINUOUS, ON-GOING IMPROVEMENT

Goals and Objectives

The goal of this session is to initiate the implementation of a system which will guide the continuous and on-going improvement of your company in the months and years ahead.

Specific objectives will be to utilize the format and agenda developed in Session 15 and offer suggestions to guide the continuation of this process.

Preparatory Information, Learning and Action

In this session you will begin implementation of your company's system of continuous, on-going improvement. At this point you and your self-managing team have an effective system and the essential tools and understanding to achieve whatever vision you choose to pursue. Now all that is needed to make it happen is on-going commitment!

It is important that you take the time to do as much preparatory work as you can to make this session a positive and productive experience. You should remind your staff to turn in issues of importance for inclusion on the agenda, distribute the agenda ahead of time, and give forethought to the what, how, who, and scheduling for the short-term action plans which will be brought up in this session.

In the last session you and your staff compiled a Top 10 Action Plan as a work agenda for Phase IV. In implementing this list, three types of involvement are possible:

- work that you as shop owner will do yourself,

- work that your staff will do (either as individuals or as a team), and

- work that you and the staff will do together.

The Best Image team decided to begin with the evaluation of the skills and learning needs of all staff members, followed by the development and implementation of an improvement program. In Session 13 and Resource Tool D we saw how the Learning Curve Continuum can be used to objectively describe fundamental competency levels for members in your staff. The Learning Curve Continuum can also be used to establish the "now" position for your staff in each area of job competency. Before you read the case study, you might review Resource Tool D in order to better understand the action taken by Best Image.

Case Study Discussion and Analysis

This case study session is a composite of several Best Image Phase IV meetings. The topics were chosen to show the variety of topics and approaches that the improvement process can involve. You should expect that your own Phase IV meetings will vary considerably from one meeting to the next.

It is important that the agenda you developed in the last session provides for review of past as well as future issues. As you can see, in this session there is considerable referral to earlier work (and earlier minutes). This will hold true for all Phase IV improvement sessions. Some sessions, of course, will not consider every agenda item.

Recommendations for Implementation

This session can be considered a model for all future Phase IV sessions. While it is important that you give careful consideration to your format and agenda before beginning these sessions, it is equally important that you don't become too rigid in their application. Central to the entire MNM Team Building Process is the concept of flexibility and willingness to modify the process, the format, and the meeting agenda to effectively meet the various challenges of change as they occur.

A final suggestion for implementing the Phase IV sessions would the importance of balancing development of new ideas and solutions with the actual implementation and monitoring of those plans. Quite simply, strategic planning without action is as ineffective as action without strategic planning.

Best Image Printing On-Going Improvement

[Unlike previous case study presentations, the Session 16 case study presented below is a composite of the proceedings from several Phase IV Best Image meetings. In choosing these examples, the effort has been made to use representative material which illustrates typical applications of the various agenda topics developed by Best Image in Session 15.]

1. *Review issues from previous meeting*

    a. *Action taken*
        - *Color copier is ordered and expected to arrive next week. We need to give serious thought in the coming weeks as to innovative ways of marketing.*
        - *The new system for processing invoices has been implemented, and is working well, particularly with respect to eliminating sources of quality errors.*
        - *Customer Service Rep A has taken over camera work, which is helping to the reduce the work load of the typesetter.*
        - *Customer Service Reps A and B have begun a staggered work schedule to provide better and longer customer service at the counter. The system appears to be working well, so far.*
        - *Nothing has been done yet with respect to pre-cutting stock.*

    b. *Problems experienced*
        - *None yet*

2. *Current positions*

    a. *Sales report*
        - *Sales for June were $41,000—fantastic!*

    b. *General market conditions*
        - *According to reports from paper salespeople,*

various miscellaneous people, and other business people, most printers are slow right now. We are not; we must doing something right!

c. Customers
   - *The Chamber of Commerce newsletter has a new format and a new contact person who will be working with us.*
   - *Trilogic Semiconductor was very, very pleased with the copying job we recently completed for them. Thanks for the great team effort!*
   - *Customer service rep A called the Greater City Church Alliance to find out why they have stopped coming in. They said that they finally bought a copier and have been using it for everything.*

3. Problem Identification and Group Problem Solving

   a. Significant or chronic problems
      - *Tagging inventory for jobs was discussed. This would involve taping the yellow part of a stock order slip to existing stock so everyone would know that stock was earmarked for a job. We currently have a problem with white bond, 60# offset, envelopes, vellum bristol—all basic stocks. We will try tagging and see if it works.*
      - *Heat from the two high-speed copiers in the front of the shop is a problem; a suggestion was made to look into having a ceiling fan installed.*
      - *Not enough time was scheduled for printing the new Precision Engineering brochure. We need to remember that when a job is too long in production, with too many gaps between stages (in this case the gaps were caused by client), continuity is lost, everyone forgets what's going on, and mistakes are made. The lesson to be learned here is that we need better communication when we have the above scenario.*

   b. Group problem solving
      - *None needed*

   c. New approaches/systems
      - *None needed*

4. Internal operations

   [In one of their Phase IV sessions, Best Image spent some time reviewing the concepts of internal customers and process path. Here they decided to discuss what each team member, as an internal customer, wanted from the department that supplies them.]

Typesetter wants:
- *as much information as possible on invoices (i.e., size, proof info, fax info, dates, logos, artwork, and photos on hand)*

Press Operators wants:
- *print size, ink color, stock, careful with abbreviations, run size notes for cutting stock oversize if bleeds (notes on outside of invoice), note if gripper is needed*
- *paper for job on hand—correct color, size, etc., and enough of it*
- *invoice in pressroom early in AM of print day*

Bindery wants:
- *to spend much less time in quality control with a goal of none needed (i.e., setups and bad copies pulled out)*
- *the right count, including enough overage*
- *jobs that are ready to go (i.e, no hair-trims, etc.)*
- *consistency in quality*
- *setups for folding, etc.*
- *"This job was printed by" tags*
- *clear due dates*
- *invoices for delivery jobs priced*

Customer Service Reps and Shop Owner want:
- *everyone to ask if something is not clear*
- *the bindery done correctly*
- *speak up when there is a problem, especially with quality*
- *pick ups and deliveries worked into schedule as quickly as possible*
- *jobs that are being picked up wrapped and on the shelf before customer comes in*

A discussion followed on ways in which these needs could be better met.

[Some of the work done under the Internal Operations agenda topic in other sessions is listed below.]

We need to remember that internal communication is extremely important, especially when two or more people become involved in one job.

It is important to note that in a small shop like ours a person's attitude effects everyone, and when we're under pressure to get a job done, that pressure effects everyone, too. The person who promises the job feels the most pressure to meet that commitment. When we're feeling really pressured, we should remember that deadlines can sometimes be moved if we ask the customer.

*We need to remember that it is very important to **meet our deadlines**. Missed deadlines typically make* *customers very unhappy and should be avoided. If it appears that we're going to miss a deadline, we could call the customer and let them know rather than have them arrive to pick up a job that's not ready.*

Our new press operator has started and is not a member of the team yet. We need to constantly remind ourselves that we need to be very much aware of this and work to help him become a part of the BI team. We need to encourage him to ask questions whenever he doesn't understand something or whenever something doesn't seem right.

5. *Quality Issues*
   - *The 60# colored papers have not been folding very well; should we switch brands?*
   - *Both high-speed copiers continue to be problematic. The old unit needs to be replaced but based on the quality problems we have been experiencing so far with the new one, we probably need to check out other options. Owner will check out what other stores are currently having good results with.*

6. *Other areas of concern*
   - *We have two special brochure jobs coming up for Precision Engineering.*
   - *Press operator B's press was scheduled for a PM but a red tag wasn't done and we failed to take the downtime into consideration when scheduling for that day.*
   - *Press operator A's press needs a major repair and until that is done he is not going to be able to print every job we throw at him. We need to try to remember his limitations and plan accordingly.*

7. *Successes*
   - *Problems don't seem to be getting us down at all!*
   - *Press operator B has been watching his language— thanks!*
   - *Bindery getting done faster—thanks!*
   - *Printed two Precision Engineering brochures without a hitch!*
   - *Customers really like pick-up and delivery service!*

8. *Other Issues*
   - *None*

Summary

With the completion of Session 16, your on-going improvement process is well underway. It's now up to you and your team to continue The MNM Process into the future. Once your staff sees that the major problems have been addressed and corrected, it would be natural for them to feel that the job has been accomplished. As owner, it's your job to make sure that this doesn't happen and you should continually strive to keep the meetings fresh, focused and productive. To demonstrate effectively that the road to excellence never ends is a major challenge and will require leadership from you.

One of the surest ways to keep your team interested in the improvement process is to provide constant feedback on the results of their efforts. Don't be afraid to let them know *often* that they're doing a great job.

Another way to keep your staff involved in the on-going improvement process is to provide access to learning materials and other resources for professional growth.

There will be times when it will become necessary to put aside the regular agenda in order to consider other issues which affect the team. Monitoring progress along the Path to the Ideal Vision, special problem solving, integrating new team members, and initiating team projects will all require special sessions and should be considered a normal part of the Phase IV work. These special issues will be considered in Chapter 14.

Now that you have completed two or three of the Phase IV on-going improvement sessions, it is time for you to begin working on Phase V.

OTHER PHASE IV ISSUES AND CONCEPTS

Most of the Phase IV meetings will follow the agenda you developed in Session 15. From time to time, however, you will find it necessary to focus on other issues which affect the entire team. These issues might include adding a new team member, the need to monitor your progress, solving a problem that surfaces, or just wanting to review the team-building process to reinforce the concept.

This chapter will deal with some of these special issues, along with other issues that affect your on-going improvement work.

Adding a New Team Member

The addition of a new member to a self-managing team will require special consideration, both on your part and on the part of the team. If the new staff member is added during the early stages of The MNM Process, all that may be needed is some extra discussion and coaching, along with a copy of the meeting minutes to date. Once the team is firmly in place, it may take a special effort on everyone's part to help the new person become an integral part of the team.

The most important part of making sure a new staff member will fit in is to strive to hire the right person. Effective Personnel Management Within a Self-Managing Team (Resource Tool G) deals with hiring new staff and writing effective classified ads. During the interview process, you should very carefully explain to all applicants about the self-managing team you have in place. By very carefully watching and listening to each applicant, you should be able to tell if someone will have difficulty with the self-managing and team concepts.

Once you have found and hired your prospective new team member, it is important that you give them as much background information as possible on the work the team has been doing. Providing a complete set of the minutes from The MNM Team Building Process is a good first step. Then you can explain the concepts of process path and internal customers, taking the new person around the path and introducing him/her to each of the team members. Then you might allow the new person to spend some time observing each of the steps in the process path and have each team member explain their function. Finally, before their first MNM meeting, you might want to explain the agenda and supply whatever background information is still needed. This will make the first MNM meeting more meaningful to your new staff member.

It is also important that you share with your team the information on your new staff member, ideally before that new person begins work. It is at this time that you need to remind your well-functioning team that the new person will know nothing about the various ways that work moves through your shop and the staff will need to be very conscientious in giving adequate explanations. Also remind them that communication will become very, very important for a while. Then, at the first meeting after the new person starts work, you can have this same discussion, and emphasize the importance of asking questions whenever anyone doesn't understand something.

Following these simple guidelines will minimize the disruption that adding a new staff member can bring about, and in a few weeks time the staff should be functioning as a team again.

Monitoring Systems

Much has already been said in this book about monitoring systems. Monitoring is an absolutely essential component of the Phase IV improvement process. Unfortunately, it's a component which is very easy to neglect.

A suggestion that will increase awareness on monitoring is to insist that when an immediate or short-term action plan and implementation schedule are worked out, a monitoring system be simultaneously developed and implemented.

Nine months after Best Image Printing conducted its "now" position ranking of the Ten Key Characteristics of the Ideal Best Image Team, they decided they needed to monitor their team building process to see if they had progressed towards their ideal vision. Using the same format as they did in Session 11, the team reevaluated the Ten Key Characteristics. Figure 14.1 shows their ranking from Session 11 along with their ranking nine months later.

Figure 14.1

TEN KEY CHARACTERISTICS OF IDEAL BEST IMAGE TEAM
9 MONTHS AFTER INITIAL RANKINGS

Characteristic	Staff Rankings	Staff Average	Owner's Ranking	
Communicative	10,8,8,7,7,7	7.8	8	
Responsible	10,7.5,9,7,9,9	8.6	8	
Skill	7,7.5,7,7,6,8,	7.1	6	Improved
Efficient	6,8.5,7,6,7,6	6.8	6	Improved
Quality	9,9,9,7,7,9	8.3	8	
Cooperative	10,9,10,8,9,10	9.3	10	
Flexible	9.5,6.5,8,8,9,10	8.5	8	
Considerate	10,7.5,9,8,8,10	8.8	10	
Positive	10,7.5,7,8,8,9	8.3	8	
Consistent	7.5,8,8,6,7,8	7.4	7	Improved
	Averages	8.1	7.9	

TEN KEY CHARACTERISTICS OF IDEAL BEST IMAGE TEAM
INITIAL RANKINGS (FROM SESSION 11)

Characteristic	Staff Rankings	Staff Average	Owner's Ranking	
Communicative	6,6,8,5,7,8	6.7	8	
Responsible	7,6,8,9,7,7	7.3	8	
Skill	6,5,7,2,7,7	5.7	5	Needs work
Efficient	6,5,7,1,6,7	5.3	5	Needs work
Quality	8,6,7,6,5,8	6.7	7	
Cooperative	6,7,8,7,8,9	7.5	10	Highest
Flexible	6,6,7,8,8,7	7.0	8	
Considerate	6,7,8,5,7,8	6.8	10	
Positive	6,6,7,5,8,7	6.5	8	
Consistent	7,5,7,8,7,8	7.0	5	Needs work
	Averages	6.7	7.4	

In comparing Best Image's new "now" position with their previous assessment, it can be seen that, overall, both the team and the owner saw improvement, and that their overall rankings are in greater alignment than they had been. In looking at the specific areas which had been identified and subsequently worked on in Task 2 (skill, efficiency, and consistency), all showed improvement.

The Best Image staff was extremely interested in finding out whether or not there had been improvement, so they were quite pleased with themselves when the results were tabulated.

To complete this particular monitoring session, the owner proceeded to take the new data and plot it on the Path to the Ideal Vision diagram. In plotting the data, the team acknowledged that the Path of Progress had not been and never would be a straight line from the "now" position to the ideal vision, but was instead an erratic line, responding to the various pressures of the change process.

Group Problem Solving

Group Problem Solving (Resource Tool F) is an ideal tool for the Phase IV improvement process. Not only will it continue to nurture the self-managing team and bring individual team members closer together, but it can result in significant breakthroughs in solving chronic problems.

Why, you say? Well, look at it this way. When you have a problem that you've encountered on the job, how do you work on it? Do you sit down and completely solve it at once? Or do you think about it off and on, over several days, including driving to and from work and at home? Most likely, you do the latter. Chances are, your staff is now thinking about problems in the same manner. During the Phase IV meetings, you'll provide an opportunity for your staff to combine their thoughts in group problem solving, and verbalizing those items that have been occupying their thoughts.

Group Problem Solving presents some of the concepts underlying the group problem solving process, an approach you might find useful for coaching team solutions to recurring problems. As is explained there, the key to problem solving is in asking the right question. In fact, once you find the right question, many times you have also found the solution!

Initiating Team Projects

At this point in The MNM Process your self-managing team should be fully functional. Now is a good time to start making better use of it! Team projects, generally involving two to four people, are a good way to utilize your team in working on tasks and problems that previously would have competed for *your* time.

One very pertinent question, of course, is when do they do it? If your shop is like most, there probably aren't enough hours in the day for them to get together. The answer, again, is overtime. But that costs money, you say. Yes, but what is *your* time worth? And aren't they doing work that *you* used to do? When you think about it that way, it's money well invested. Another benefit of team projects is that for every hour they are engaged in this joint task or problem solving mode on their own, you can bet your self-managing team is getting stronger and stronger. So don't worry about the overtime, it'll be paid back many times over!

Aligning Your Immediate and Short-Term Action Plans With Your Long-Term Strategies

You have already spent considerable time developing preliminary long-term strategies (Phase II). In Phase V you will develop final long-term strategies which will utilize all of the sessions to guide your work into the future. Therefore, as you progress though the Phase IV sessions, it is essential that you constantly check to assure that your immediate and short-term action plans are in alignment with your long-term strategies. This can be done either by you alone or together with your team; the choice is yours. The option you choose, however, is clearly secondary to ensuring that the monitoring gets done.

Discrepancies in alignment will, of course, require correction. Before doing so, you should carefully review both the short-term action plans *and* the long-term strategies to see which is deficient. Often, group problem solving and brainstorming sessions with your staff will come up with some surprisingly innovative ideas. To assume that the long-term strategy is always correct would go against the concept of continuous and on-going improvement.

Integration of Phase IV and Phase V Work

In the next chapter we'll look at Phase V—formalizing your long-term strategy. It is essential that this work be closely aligned and totally integrated with the Phase IV work. By integrated we mean that there are no contradictions or conflicts between the work that you are doing on your own in Phase V and the work that your team is doing along with you in Phase IV.

How do you know the two phases are integrated? Some owners, because of their management style, will be willing to share most, if not all, of the Phase V work with their team. For companies such as these the integration can be regularly monitored just like any other part of the process. For the owner who doesn't feel comfortable in sharing as much of his/her long-term plans, the task is more difficult in that it requires looking in the "queen's mirror" again. By this time in the process, hopefully, your mirror is much more accurate than it has been.

■

ON-GOING

STRATEGIC

WORK

CHAPTER 15

IMPROVEMENT IS A CONTINUAL PROCESS

Phase V is an on-going monitoring process which utilizes feedback from the company's immediate and short-term action plans to suggest or mandate changes in the long-term visions and strategies. Phase V goes hand in hand with Phase IV—if Phase IV *implements* the on-going improvement cycle, then Phase V *perpetuates* it. The interplay between these two concurrent phases is dynamic and constant, and it is your responsibility to continually make sure they are in agreement.

Phase V of The MNM Process can be started any time after the second session of Phase IV (Session 16). By this time, the Phase IV process should be understood well enough by you and your team that you can once again turn your attention to the long-term issues facing your business. You will be doing the work of Phase V on your own. However, it will be quite different from the work you did in Phases I and II as you will be constantly referencing and integrating all of the thoughts and ideas generated in Phase III and those which will continue to come from Phase IV. The work of this phase can be done at any time that it is convenient. You should be as conscientious in scheduling the work of this phase as you have been in scheduling the work of Phases III and IV.

In this chapter we will learn how Phase IV and Phase V are closely interrelated in a dynamic way, as Cycles of On-Going Improvement (see figure 16.1). Before discussing these cycles of improvement, we will review some of the general concepts and ideas that were presented in Phases I and II. Many of these concepts should now have greater meaning for you then when they were first introduced.

In Chapter 16 we will look at how the owner of Best Image Printing revised his preliminary long-term strategies so that they were in alignment with the ideas and concepts that evolved from the Phase III and Phase IV work.

Review of Phase I

We began Phase I of The MNM Team Building Process by considering the basic concepts of mission and vision, and ended by creating a mission statement and an overall vision statement for your company.

You should take some time here to review the mission statement you prepared in Chapter 6. How does it sound to you now? Is it still appropriate? Is it adequate? If not, this is the time to modify it. Whether or not it needs changing is not important. What is important is that your company has a formal mission statement which clearly and succinctly states the special purpose of your business as you presently see it.

Chapter 7 focused on developing an overall ideal vision of the long-term future of your company. To accomplish this objective, you developed separate visions for the eight basic component parts of your business (products and services, customers, physical facilities, equipment, staff personnel, vendors, marketing and sales, competition). You should now review each of those component visions. How do they look to you now? Is your perspective the same or has it changed? After you have reviewed all eight individual visions, go back through them and make any modifications that you feel are necessary in order to bring the visions into alignment with your current perspective of the overall vision of your company.

In considering the work you did in Chapter 7, it is important to remember that this eight-fold compartmentalization of your business, while useful for focusing your attention and facilitating action, has a fundamental limitation. This limitation is that *no single component ever exists by itself, but is closely connected to each of the other parts to make up the whole of your business.*

Unfortunately, when problems arise in one area of a business, connections to other components are often forgotten, and as a result, short-term action plans to deal with the crisis at hand are frequently at odds with the overall long-term vision. During such crises, if the individual component visions are not consistent with one another, then the immediate problem is compounded. Recognizing this problem, it is important that once you are satisfied with the content of the eight individual visions, you focus on the relationship of each of the eight visions to each other. Are they consistent? Or do they conflict in certain areas? In some cases, the consistency or conflict is easy to see; in other cases, it is more difficult.

There is a useful, versatile and simple technique that you can use to check the consistency and effect of one vision or strategy upon another. This technique is the Correlation Matrix (figure 15.1). This matrix can be used in virtually any situation where you want to check the degree of interconnection between two or more variables.

The Correlation Matrix compares 16 vision components chosen at random from the Best Image Printing visions in Chapter 7. In the matrix, the 16 components are plotted against one another to show their interconnection.

As shown by an analysis of the Correlation Matrix, it can provide a qualitative and fairly reliable understanding of the effect of various vision components on each other. The process can be done in a short time and is effective in identifying areas of conflicting vision and, subsequently, conflicting strategy. Had the example shown negative effects between vision components, then this would have been considered a red flag leading to further investigation and, if necessary, revision of one or more of the vision components.

When you are satisfied that your vision components and overall vision are in alignment and are consistent with your current perspective of your business, you should go on to review Phase II.

Review of Phase II

We began Phase II by considering several guiding principles for use in developing your company's preliminary overall long-term strategy. These principles included personal management and decision making styles, self-managing teams, internal customers, and total quality systems. At this time it would be useful to look at each of these concepts again relative to changes that have taken place at your company.

When you first read the section in Chapter 8 on management styles, you were asked to examine the Management Style Choices presented in figure 8.1 and determine which was your management style at that time. Perhaps the first obvious question to ask now is, Has your management style changed in the past several months, and if so, how? Assuming that a change has occurred, if you think back over the meetings of Phases III and IV, do you observe a gradual change or can you think of a particular session or experience that triggered a more sudden change?

How about your staff? How have they responded to the challenge of change, specifically as it relates to accepting the additional responsibility and accountability that goes along with being a part of a self-managing team? Probably you have seen a lot of change in your staff. And if your team is like most, the growth in this area has been quite different from one staff member to the next.

One of the issues that is likely to come up at some point is what to do with a non-team player. This problem is addressed in Resource Tool G,

Figure 15.1 ■ **CORRELATION MATRIX OF VISION COMPONENTS FOR BEST IMAGE PRINTING**

This Correlation Matrix shows the degree of interconnection between the various components of Best Image Printing's Ideal Vision.

The diagram is read as follows: If any one of the numbered vision components in rows 1-16 is implemented, it will have a positive (+), neutral (0) or negative (–) effect on achieving the lettered vision component in columns A-P.

For example: If an additional high speed copier is added (#7), it will have a positive effect on increasing gros by 25% (M).

VISION COMPONENT

1.	A	Expand into color copying & imaging
2.	B	Expand high-speed copying capability
3.	C	Expand bindery capability
4.	D	Expand customer base by 20%; recession proof
5.	E	Expand space by 250 sq. ft.
6.	F	Upgrade existing space inside & outside
7.	G	Add additional high-speed copier
8.	H	Add new color computer system
9.	I	Develop preventive maintenance schedule
10.	J	Develop self-managing work teams
11.	K	Develop on-going training/cross-training program
12.	L	Establish stronger relationships with vendors
13.	M	Increase gross sales by 25%
14.	N	Add 5 new market segments to customer base
15.	O	Understand printing capabilities of competition
16.	P	Learn customers likes & dislikes about competition

DEGREE OF INTERCONNECTION

	A	B	C	D	E	F	G	H	I	J	K	L	M	N	O	P	(+s)
1.		0	0	+	0	+	0	+	0	0	0	+	+	+	0	0	6
2.	0		0	+	0	+	+	0	0	0	0	+	+	+	0	0	6
3.	+	+		+	0	+	+	+	0	0	0	0	+	+	0	0	8
4.	+	+	0		0	0	+	+	0	0	0	+	+	+	0	0	7
5.	+	+	+	+		+	+	+	0	0	0	0	+	+	0	0	9
6.	+	+	+	+	0		+	+	+	0	0	0	+	+	0	0	9
7.	0	+	0	+	0	0		0	0	0	0	+	+	+	0	0	5
8.	+	0	0	+	0	0	0		0	0	0	+	+	+	0	0	5
9.	+	+	+	+	0	0	0	0		+	+	+	+	0	0	0	8
10.	+	+	+	+	0	+	0	0	+		+	+	+	+	+	+	12
11.	+	+	+	+	0	+	0	0	+	+		+	+	+	0	0	10
12.	+	+	0	0	0	0	+	+	0	0	0		+	+	+	+	8
13.	+	+	+	+	+	+	+	+	0	0	+	0		+	0	0	10
14.	+	+	0	+	0	0	0	0	0	0	0	0	0		+	+	5
15.	+	+	+	+	0	0	0	0	+	+	+	+	+	+		+	11
16.	+	+	0	+	0	+	0	+	0	+	+	0	+	+	+		10
(+s)	13	13	7	14	1	8	7	8	4	4	5	9	14	14	4	4	

Figure 15.1 continued

HOW TO READ THE CORRELATION MATRIX

The Correlation Matrix shows the degree of interconnection between various vision components of Best Image Printing's Ideal Vision.

In looking at the diagram, the following results and conclusions can be drawn:

1. None of the vision components have a negative effect on any of the other vision components. This indicates that the individual components are in alignment with each other and provide a consistent overall vision.

2. If each of the 16 vision components were pursued, the individual components having *the greatest positive effect on the rest of the combined vision* would be:

row 10	develop self-managing team (12+)
row 11	develop on-going training program (10+)
row 13	increase gross sales by 25% (10+)
row 16	learn what customers like and dislike about competition (10+)

3. If all of the 16 vision components were pursued, then the individual components which would be *most positively affected by the other components* would be:

column D	expand customer base by 20% (14+)
column M	increase sales by 25% (14+)
column N	add 5 new market segments to customer base (14+)

4. Similarly, if we add the plusses of the corresponding number and letter together, we obtain a relative ranking of the *overall degree of interconnection between the 16 components.*

   Thus, 13-M (increase gross sales by 25%) is *most related* to other components of the overall vision, and 5-E (expand space by 250 sq. ft.) is *least related* to other vision components.

Effective Personnel Management within a Self-Managing Team. Most people, even if they have never had the opportunity to work in a team situation, will, over a period of time, become comfortable with the self-managing team concepts. Some, however, will not, and eventually other action may become necessary. Suggestions for dealing with these more difficult cases, as well as with the whole issue of recruiting new team members, are presented in Resource Tool G.

As head coach and resource for the self-managing team, one of your most challenging responsibilities is to know when to take action yourself and when to let the team work it out. The only suggestion that can be offered is to allow enough time for the team to work out problems themselves. Remember, this is a difficult yet important transition for your entire team, including yourself. So, again, give it time.

By now the concept of internal customers should be thoroughly understood. Here again, some staff members will grasp the idea enthusiastically and *implement* it, while others will only *think* about it. As chief change agent, another of your responsibilities is continuing to help your staff move concepts into practice. One way of doing this is to periodically reintroduce a concept, in the on-going Phase IV work, to illustrate solutions to problems with which the team may be struggling. Internal customers is a powerful concept that can solve many routine issues.

While many companies today are actively introducing total quality systems, there is still much debate as to the right approach. The MNM Process approaches the concept from the conviction that producing quality is essentially a function of doing the right thing; that is, give your staff the understanding of what the customer requires and provide a work environment that nurtures the employee to do the right thing and you *will* have quality. While statistical approaches can help improve quality by identifying hidden sources of "non-quality," ultimately it comes down to people and pride in workmanship. To illustrate the point, look again at the nine month monitoring of Best Image with respect to quality in figure 14.1. In comparing the two rankings, it can be seen that the average of the individual team member's evaluation of quality rose by 1.6 points. Although there had been some direct changes made in the process path to improve quality during the Phase III work, the biggest improvements in quality can be attributed to the overall self-managing team approach which provided individuals with the opportunity to correct sources of quality inconsistency, thus encouraging a much higher level of personal awareness and pride in workmanship.

Following the discussion of guiding principles, the remainder of Phase II focused on developing preliminary long-term strategies for achieving the vision components identified in Phase I.

CHAPTER 16

REVISING YOUR PRELIMINARY STRATEGIES

In this chapter you will conduct a systematic review of each of the preliminary long-term strategies which you developed in Phase II, and then (if necessary) formally revise your overall strategy so that it is in alignment with your current mission and vision. To prepare yourself for this work, you should go back and carefully review all of the minutes from the Phase III and Phase IV work to date.

Once you have completed your review of the Phase III and Phase IV work, go through each of the preliminary strategies you developed in Phase II and consider the following questions for each element, goal or objective of the strategy.

- Considering the present company position and situation relative to the combined experience from the Phase III and Phase IV work, should this element, goal or objective be retained as part of a viable and effective strategy for achieving the company's vision as it now stands?

- If the strategic element, goal, or objective is to be retained, does it need to be modified in any way? If so, how?

- Are there new strategic elements, goals, or objectives that could be added to make the overall strategy more effective?

As you review your preliminary strategies, you will probably find that many are quite deficient and in need of revision. This is to be expected, and as you revise these strategies, you should go about it in a formal manner, putting your plans down on paper in as complete a format as possible. This work is critically important since *it is this long-term strategy which will serve to guide the overall development of your company until such time as you feel the need to revise your vision and strategy again.*

In making these revisions, you should use the formats which were provided in Phase II where you think they are appropriate. However, don't feel that you are in any way bound to them. They are presented as starting points and you are encouraged to expand on them.

To provide some examples of the revisioning process, we will look at Best Image Printing's preliminary strategies developed in Chapter 7 and reexamine them in terms of Best Image's Phase III and Phase IV experiences.

Revisions to Best Image Printing's Long-Term Strategies

Products and Services

Analysis of the Best Image preliminary long-term strategy for products and services revealed several areas that needed revision:

1. The acquisition of a third press and hiring of a new press operator was delayed for a year to allow the self-managing team to settle in. *Because of the increased efficiency of the staff, all orders were being processed through the shop on time, and it seemed appropriate to test the limits of the existing system before expanding.*

2. The purchase of a color copier was made a short-term action. *Because of the Phase III discussions, the owner decided that the purchase of the color copier should be done immediately, rather than waiting. In listening to input from the staff, it was obvious that there was a strategic advantage to getting one right away.*

3. The decision was made to immediately begin offering pickup and delivery. *Based on the staff's comments in the Phase III sessions, the owner (who had not considered the idea at all) decided that the implementation of free pick-up and delivery offered great strategic advantage and should be implemented immediately.*

Customers

Analysis of the Best Image preliminary long-term strategy for customers demonstrated exceptionally close alignment between perceived short-term and long-term needs. For the most part, the revisions to the preliminary long-term strategy focused on speeding up the implementation of several of the objectives noted in the long-term strategy.

1. The development and implementation of a new, comprehensive marketing plan was made an immediate priority. *One of the most obvious conclusions of Phase III was that Best Image really did provide good products and service, and that the problem was not competition, but rather that many businesses did not know about them. Consequently, although the proposed goal of expanding the customer*

base by 20% in the preliminary long-term strategy remained, the implementation process was moved up.

2. The polling of customers to evaluate the effective-ness of current products and services was made a short-term priority. *Much of the work of Phase III validated the proposed long-term goal of increasing the percentage of repeat customers. However, the work showed that not only was there value to be gained in polling lost customers, but existing customers should be considered an extensive source of information regarding the effectiveness of current products and services.*

Physical Facilities

Analysis of the Best Image preliminary long-term strategy for physical facilities demonstrated that the need for acquiring additional space was definitely a long-term concern, but at present the company should focus on maximizing its current operation and facilities.

1. Because the decision to purchase a third press was delayed for a year, converting the storage room to accommodate the platemaker was also delayed. *At the end of the Phase III experience, it was obvious to the owner that for the foreseeable future Best Image's greatest strategic advantage would be to focus its improvement efforts on improving staff capabilities, building the team, and maximizing the utilization of existing facilities and equipment. Converting the storage room did not realistically fit into this plan.*

Equipment

Analysis of the Best Image preliminary long-term strategy for equipment demonstrated close alignment between the preliminary long-term and short-term needs. As was discussed under products and services, some changes were made in the long-term strategy with respect to capital equipment purchases. Another revision included:

1. The development and implementation of a preven-tive maintenance system for equipment was made a priority short-term strategy. *One of the early conclusions from the implementation of the self-managing team was that its effectiveness was directly related to the degree that the equipment could be relied upon to deliver dependable and sustained high production and quality. Once the implications of this fact were understood and appreciated by the team, it was obvious that a preventive maintenance system should be implemented immediately.*

Staff

Analysis of the Best Image preliminary long-term strategy for staff showed major deficiencies in terms of a meaningful long-term strategy. Accordingly, numerous additions and revisions were made, some of which included:

1. The implementation of Phase IV of The MNM Process would continue indefinitely. *At this point it was obvious to all that The MNM Process was producing excellent results on many fronts, especially the self-managing team. There was no question in anyone's mind that the Phase IV Improvement Process should continue indefinitely.*

2. The implementation of a comprehensive, on-going training program for each staff member would begin as soon as the plan was developed and would continue indefinitely. *The Phase IV work identified the development of an on-going skill and learning improvement program as having very high priority. A short-term action plan was developed to conduct a comprehensive study of existing skill and learning needs for each job function and staff member. Once these needs could be assessed, a long-term action plan would need to be developed to schedule the necessary training and education during the months ahead.*

3. A comprehensive personnel policy would be developed to reflect the guidelines and concepts of The MNM Process. *As a result of the changes in staff responsibility and accountability that were developing as a result of the implementation of The MNM Process, the owner realized that it was necessary to develop a personnel policy which would serve as a guide for existing staff, as well as for staff that would join the team in the future.*

4. No staff would be added for at least 12 months. *It became increasingly obvious to the owner that his staff was capable of much more than they had been doing. More work was being produced less stressfully and with fewer problems than had been prior to the meetings. And turn-around times had noticeably decreased. The staff was working together more cooperatively than they had been, and it appeared that additional personnel would be unnecessary for some time.*

Vendors

Analysis of the Best Image preliminary long-term strategy for vendors demonstrated close alignment between preliminary long-term and short-term needs. As the work of Phase III and IV had not turned up any significantly different ideas or approaches, the preliminary long-term strategy was allowed to stand as previously developed. Once this decision was made, then, the owner went to work on the details of implementing the strategy.

Marketing and Sales

Analysis of the Best Image preliminary long-term strategy for marketing and sales demonstrated close alignment between preliminary long-term and short-term needs. As a result of the Phase III meetings it was obvious that the staff had many useful ideas to contribute in the area of marketing and sales, particularly by providing feedback on the effectiveness of the marketing program. Accordingly, some modifications and revisions were made to the preliminary long-term marketing and sales strategy, including:

1. Staff members should become more involved in the marketing and sales component of the business. *Prior to The MNM Process experience, the owner had personally developed all of the company's strategy on marketing and sales. After considering the ideas and insight which had developed during the Phase III and IV meetings, however, he decided that it would be worthwhile to involve at least some of the staff in more of the planning. This involvement would take place as part of the on-going Phase IV work, as well as through delegated team projects.*

Competition

Analysis of the Best Image preliminary long-term strategy for marketing and sales demonstrated close alignment between preliminary long-term and short-term needs. This is another area where the staff had contributed many useful ideas on the issue of competition in the Phase III meetings. For the most part, the preliminary long-term strategy was acceptable; however, the owner once again thought that greater input from the staff would be useful. Consequently, some modifications were made to the preliminary strategy, including:

1. Use staff instead of an outside consultant to conduct an on-going marketing survey of businesses regarding attitudes, preferences and complaints about existing printing services in town. *Based on the interest and understanding of the primary issues demonstrated by the team in the Phase III work regarding the issue of competition, the owner decided that it would be worthwhile for Best Image to initiate the market survey itself. The approach would be to utilize team input from Phase IV meetings to generate a questionnaire and then conduct a telephone survey of businesses on a scheduled, long-term basis.*

Figure 16.1 ■ **PHASES IV & V CYCLES OF ON-GOING IMPROVEMENT**

This diagram illustrates how Phases IV and V work together to produce "Cycles of On-Going Improvement." By using these cycles it is possible to provide your company with appropriate guidance and direction on a continuous basis.

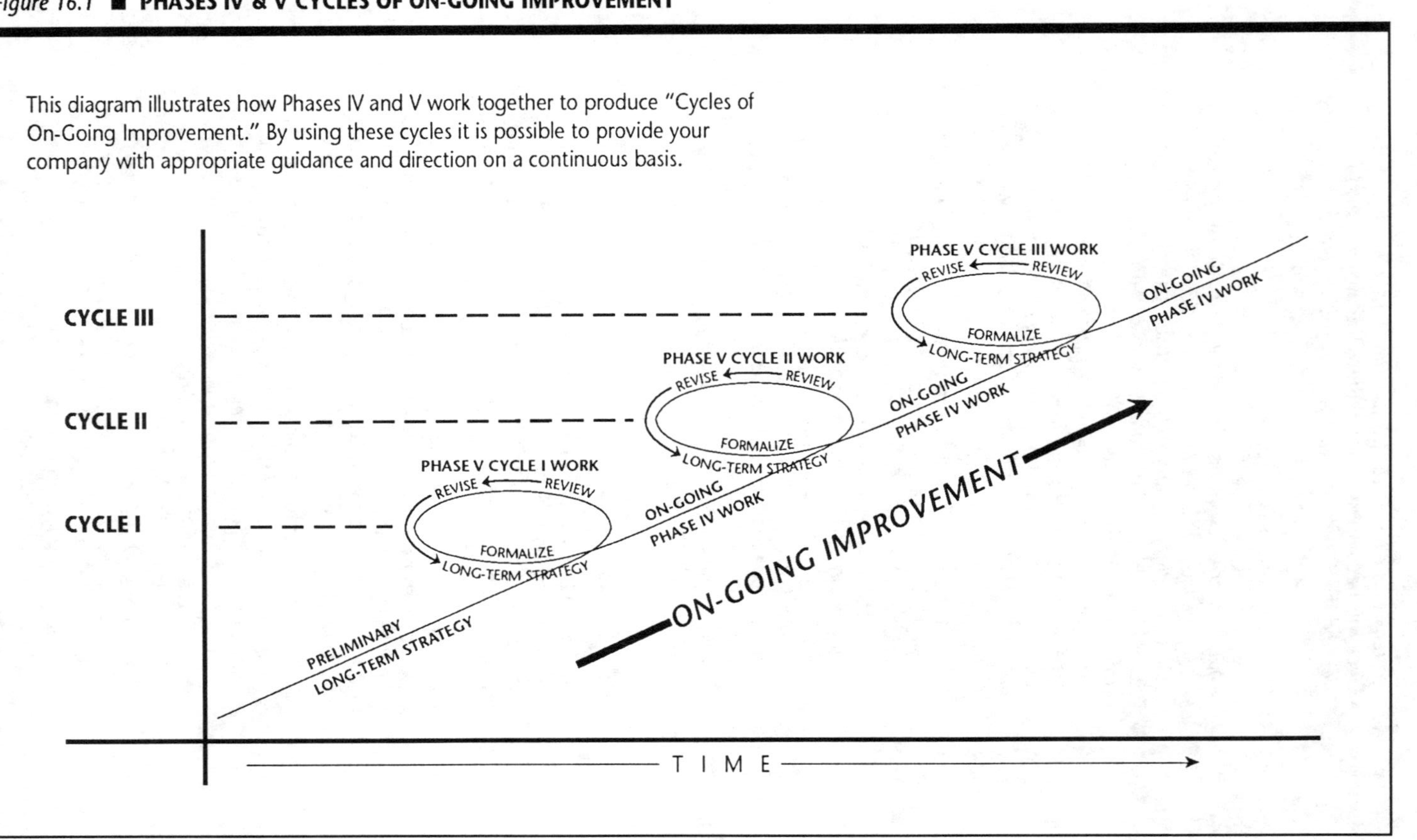

2. Develop and implement an on-going staff awareness and information gathering program to gather
   up-to-date information on the competition. *This
   strategy is based on the concept that almost every day
   each staff member comes in contact with information
   which could provide insight on Best Image's position
   relative to the competition. The objective of this long-
   term strategy would be to provide a format which
   would allow this information to be put to best use.*

On-Going Improvement and Revisioning

The Phase IV and V Cycles of On-Going Improvement are diagrammed in figure 16.1. As shown in the diagram, Cycle I can be considered finished when your review and revisioning of the eight preliminary long-term strategies is complete, and you are confident there are no remaining deficiencies, inconsistencies, or contradictions between your new long-term strategies and the work generated in Phases III and IV. At this point you can once again turn your attention to the on-going Phase IV improvement work as you apply the Cycle I long-term strategies to guide and focus your efforts.

Inevitably, at some point in the future, you will once again begin to notice inconsistencies and deficiencies cropping up between the Cycle 1 long-term strategies and the work coming out of the Phase IV improvement meetings. These inconsistencies and deficiencies are a signal that it is time again to go through the Phase V process and review and revise your long-term strategies, just as you did in Cycle 1. This review and revisioning will, of course, result in new Cycle 2 long-term strategies which will now guide your Phase IV work.

Looking at figure 16.1, you can see how the Cycles of On-Going Improvement can continue to provide your company with up-to-date guidance and direction for as long as you choose to apply the process.

CONCLUSION

The End is Only the Beginning ...

Frequently we hear how all good things must come to an end. In the case of The MNM Team Building Process, though, the end *is* only the beginning ... the beginning of an on-going process of improvement which will benefit you, your staff, and your company for as long as you choose to pursue it.

If you have just finished reading The MNM Process for the first time, we hope that the material has been useful and interesting, and most importantly, we hope that it will serve as an inspiration to you as you implement your own program!

If you are reading The MNM Process for the second time, then you've probably just completed Cycle I of the Phase IV and V Cycles of On-Going Improvement. In that case, congratulations! And may your Cycles of On-Going Improvement continue to unfold as you would like them to!

RESOURCES

■

THE
TOOL
KIT

THE TOOL KIT

The MNM Process Tool Kit has been designed to provide better understanding of the concepts, techniques and ideas which you will be using throughout The MNM Process. In preparing the Tool Kit, the objective has been to introduce only the minimum amount of theory necessary to effectively implement these ideas and concepts. Many readers will find that this material is all they'll ever need. For more curious readers, however, the Tool Kit also provides references to secondary sources and related topics which would prove useful in future work in the improvement process.

Contents of The MNM Process Tool Kit

RESOURCE TOOL A

PREFERENCES IN THINKING STYLES: A KEY TO BETTER BUSINESS

This tool provides a basic understanding of two primary thinking styles and how individual preferences in thinking style can affect every aspect of your company's business relationship, including staff, customers and vendors. It includes a 15-minute, self-administered Brain Preference Profile which, when completed, can be quickly put to use in improving internal communication, customer service, productivity, quality, and numerous other issues.

RESOURCE TOOL B

STRATEGIC FUTURING: A TECHNIQUE FOR PREDICTING HIGHLY PROBABLE OUTCOMES

The future can never be totally predictable. This Tool, however, enables you and your staff to systematically explore business trends and options in order to predict the most probable outcomes and resulting events. In short, Strategic Futuring allows you to develop meaningful contingency plans in advance, and anticipate your vulnerability in worst case scenarios.

RESOURCE TOOL C

PATH TO THE IDEAL VISION

The Path to the Ideal Vision concept is the essence of The MNM Process. This Tool provides an overview of the process in generic form and shows how you can apply the concept to any business goal or objective that you would like to achieve.

RESOURCE TOOL D

THE LEARNING CURVE CONTINUUM

This Tool provides an understanding of the continuum in human learning. Using this concept, it is possible to map out effective short-term and long-term strategies to guide the training and learning activities of your company.

RESOURCE TOOL E

MINDSTORMING: A GROUP PROCESS FOR MORE EFFECTIVE BRAINSTORMING

Group brainstorming for ideas can often result in important new insight and innovation just when you need it most. Mindstorming offers an effective way of enhancing the effectiveness of the group process, while simultaneously encouraging ever greater participation of group members.

RESOURCE TOOL F

GROUP PROBLEM SOLVING

This Tool considers the basic elements of group problem solving and offers suggestions to lead you and your team to faster and more focused problem solving.

RESOURCE TOOL G

EFFECTIVE PERSONNEL MANAGEMENT WITHIN A SELF-MANAGING TEAM

The primary goal of The MNM Process is to develop your staff into a highly productive and quality conscious self-managing team. Achieving this team, and maintaining it once it is formed, will require substantial on-going work on the part of the owner. This tool provides you with some helpful suggestions, including how to deal with a reluctant team member and how to hire new team members.

RESOURCE TOOL H

BOOKS YOU MIGHT WANT TO READ

This Tool provides a list of reading materials for curious people.

PREFERENCES IN THINKING STYLES: A KEY TO BETTER BUSINESS

About 15 years ago, there was a flurry of activity in scientific circles as researchers began focusing on the intriguing new discovery that the left and right sides of the brain (which are connected by a thick bundle of nerve fibers called the *corpus callosum*) apparently go about perceiving and processing data from the outside world in fundamentally different ways. In 1981, Dr. Roger Sperry, a psychobiologist in California, received a Nobel Prize for research in this area. This work demonstrated convincingly that the two hemispheres of the brain did indeed demonstrate important functional differences, and that for certain kinds of tasks one side of the brain was better suited to accomplishing the task than was the other. The outcome of this work, and the vast amount of research to follow, resulted in what came to be commonly known as the right and left brain processing theory.

Today, more than 20 years after the first discoveries, research in left and right brain processing continues to provide major breakthroughs in understanding how and why we humans think the way we do. (For the latest summary of this work, an excellent book is *Left Brain, Right Brain* 3rd ed. by Springer and Deutsch.) It is now known, for example, that the picture is much more complicated than first proposed—namely that many, if not most, tasks require input from both the left *and* right hemispheres, as opposed to always having a clear and sharp separation of the two functions, as initially thought. Balanced and on-going communication between the two hemispheres across the corpus callosum is increasingly seen as the norm and the desired state, rather than a highly lateralized state to either the left or the right. But despite the fact that the mystery continues to become more complex as more data comes in, the concept of left and right specialization has held up remarkably well under the immense scientific scrutiny it has received, and several specializations in function are now fairly well agreed upon. Figure A.1 presents a general summary of these specialized functions of the left and right hemispheres.

This research was found to have application in non-scientific walks of life. Artists found in the work important keys to unlocking creativity. Betty Edwards, for example, in her book *Drawing on the Right Side of the Brain,* was able to couple these ideas with her experience to develop a method of drawing which could teach beginners to draw with incredible success. Educators such as Joseph Bogen realized that here at last was a way of understanding, reaching, teaching and achieving excellence with many young people who previously were routinely categorized as problem students.

Inevitably the business world began to pick up on the implications. Madison Avenue, for example, was quick to see the implications of the work in advertising, and numerous ads began to appear on television and in magazines which either openly or covertly played upon the left and right brain specializations. Saab, for example, ran a highly successful two-page ad in which one panel, entitled a car for the right-brain, showed a provocative picture of one of their cars swooping down a mountain road. The other panel, entitled a car for the left brain, consisted of only tightly written, highly technical copy complete with detailed performance statistics. In other areas, big business management found that the concepts provided important tools for more successful decision making. As David Loy explains in his book, *The Sphinx and the Rainbow,* apparently our "best" decisions result when there is consensus between the left and right hemispheres; when the hemispheres are in conflict, the decision is more likely to be a poor one.

How, you are probably thinking, does this fit in with The MNM Process, and what good is it to me and my staff? Well, the short answer is simply that it fits in many, many ways! Specifically, however, we'll restrict our attention to the following two objectives:

- Understanding thinking style preference as a key to greater internal and external customer communication and satisfaction.

- Matching your brain to your job, or how to recognize which job functions and tasks are best suited for your staff members and potential staff members.

Resource Tool A uses the term "preferences in thinking styles" because, as it turns out, most of us *do* prefer to use certain styles of thinking. In figure A.1, the terms "Type A" and "Type B" thinking styles are correlated with some of the traits commonly associated with the specialized functions of the left and right hemispheres. Research will undoubtedly modify our current understanding of left and right brain function, but as humans, we will still continue to show preferences in thinking styles. In that respect, Type A and Type B traits, as presented, offer convenient and meaningful categories.

Figure A.1

PREFERENCES IN THINKING STYLES
AS RELATED TO LEFT BRAIN, RIGHT BRAIN SPECIALIZATION

During the past 15 years, research in a variety of fields has focused on determining how, and to what degree, the left and right brain hemispheres are specialized and lateralized for different mental functions. Research continues in this area to better define the nature and limits of this specialization and lateralization.

For many of the traits listed below, there is significant data which would support them as being more dominantly associated with one side of the brain than with the other. Other research shows that some traits are less lateralized than others and that both sides may play a role, but with one side being more dominant.

Regardless of *where* these functions take place, however, there is no question that the two columns represent two different types of thinking, knowing or processing styles. In studying these two columns, you will note that the traits are arranged as *opposites* of one another, making it possible to use these two lists in a practical way to describe Personal Preferences in Thinking Styles.

| TYPE A THINKING STYLES | TYPE B THINKING STYLES |
Left Brain Traits	Right Brain Traits
Verbal	Non verbal/visual/spatial
Analytical/logical	Intuitive/spontaneous
Linear	Holistic
Literal/explicit	Symbolic/metaphoric
Temporal/short term	Timeless/long-term
Objective	Subjective
Mathematical	Artistic/musical
Sequential	Synthesis/simultaneous
Concrete/"Bottom Line"	Imaginative/dreamer
Rational	Emotional
Digital	Analogic
Western thought	Eastern thought
	Sexual
	Spiritual

The point is that you can *use* these concepts without going into all the scientific jargon, just as you can drive a car without understanding how all the parts work. If you look again at figure A.1, you will see that the left and right columns are arranged in *pairs of opposites,* and many of us will, *overall,* tend to fall more into one column than the other. Try it. Which column best describes the way you think? In doing this simple exercise you have, in a crude way, established your thinking style preference. However, to provide you and your staff with a more definitive method of establishing your thinking style,

The MNM Process Thinking Style Preference Profile is included as a key part of Resource Tool A.

The Thinking Style Preference Profile will require about 15 minutes to take. Each of the questions in the profile is based on the results of research in left and right brain processing and has been carefully developed to give an accurate understanding of your thinking style preference. Go ahead and complete the profile now, following the instructions exactly as given. When you are done, score your profile, using the instructions provided.

Feel free to copy the profile and give it to your staff. The following sections discuss how you can now use your profile results, and those of your staff, in addressing the two objectives proposed above.

Thinking Style Preferences as a Key to Internal and External Customer Communication and Satisfaction

We have all had the frustrating experience of trying to communicate with a customer or staff member where, no matter how hard each person tried, the results were totally unsuccessful. In a similar vein, we frequently will use or hear the expressions "I don't know were you're coming from," "so what's your point; no, it's not clear!", "can you draw me a picture or show me what it will look like?", "I hear what you're saying, but it doesn't mean anything to me," and so on.

Situations and expressions such as these quite commonly can be traced to differences in thinking styles. As shown in figure A.1, the Type A thinker tends to be verbal, literal, and bottom line, as opposed to corresponding Type B thinker characteristics of visual, metaphoric, and imaginative. Obviously, if you put together two people who tend to be strongly lateralized and opposite in their thinking styles (say a 13A/123A and a 18B/129B), they are going to have a very difficult time in communicating! And this occurs often.

So what do you do? Let's say you have a very sharp, efficient customer service rep who is 13A/123A, and an important customer who from your experience is a classic Type B. What are your options? If you know your thinking style and the styles of your staff, perhaps you could let one of your more Type B people deal with that customer. Another possibility would be to have the customer service rep focus on giving the kind of language and communication that the customer needs and wants. This is not as hard as it sounds, and with minimal practice you can become quite skilled. We all know how to use both sides of our brain; some of us just prefer not to—until, however, we see value in it! The third option, and the one which is ultimately the best choice, is to have a customer service rep whose thinking style is *by nature* more balanced and who can readily implement the appropriate thinking style. And how do you achieve this? Very simple: you *hire* them! In Resource Tool G you'll see some simple employment ads that will attract that person.

Matching Your Company's Thinking Style to the Job At Hand

Most people have areas of skills and abilities that are easier to acquire and master than others. In many cases these skills and occupational abilities can be traced directly to thinking style preferences. It is also true that many job functions or tasks are definitely more closely aligned with the characteristics of one thinking style than the other. Unfortunately, in many businesses the match between people and job function is given much less consideration than it should be.

Exercise 2 presents a method whereby job functions and tasks within your shop can be analyzed in terms of required thinking styles and then matched with the natural thinking style preferences of your people. Many times simply understanding this match (or mis-match, as the case may be) is sufficient to begin improving the situation (as we saw in option two above for the mismatched customer service rep and customer). However, in chronic problem areas it may require long-term training, on-going work, or occasionally an actual change in personnel.

There are two ways of approaching Exercise 2. One way is basically a Type A thinking style approach where you systematically go through each of your staff positions and, using the techniques and instructions provided, come up with an overall job function thinking style ranking. Then you can compare this ranking with the thinking style preference of the staff person who is responsible for working in this area. This approach is quite objective and provides *real* numbers. A Type B thinking style approach, which is definitely more subjective but takes considerably less time, is to simply consider each of the job functions in terms of the two columns in figure A.1 and then estimate an overall ranking on a scale of 1 to 10 as to whether the job is primarily Type A or Type B in nature, and compare this ranking with the person assigned to the job. Your choice of method, of course, will depend on *your* thinking style preference!

Exercise 1

THINKING STYLE PREFERENCE PROFILE

© 1989 Michael P. O'Connor

NAME: ____ DATE: ___________

JOB FUNCTION: ____

PART I

The 20 questions in this profile are designed to indicate personal preferences in brain utilization and thinking styles. There are no "right" or "wrong" answers.

In Part I, please check the appropriate box for *either A or B* for each question. *You cannot answer both.* If you have trouble in doing this, pick the answer which seems to fit you best.

Do not read or start Part II until you have finished Part I.

1. In finding a destination in an unfamiliar town:

    ☐ ____ A. I need to have explicit directions before going, and once there, rely on street maps, numbers and names to find my destination.

    ☐ ____ B. I am content in having only a general location of my destination, knowing that once I am in the general area I'll be able to find it without much trouble.

2. In decision making:

    ☐ ____ A. I prefer to take the time to carefully evaluate all options, perhaps listing advantages or disadvantages.

    ☐ ____ B. I tend to come to a decision all of a sudden without really thinking about it.

3. The company that you work for has just opened two new divisions. As a long-term employee, you are being offered a senior position in the division of your choice. Considering your past experience and present skills, which of the two positions listed below would you be best suited for?

    ☐ ____ A. Data management and product inventory control.

    ☐ ____ B. Advertising design and layout.

4. In terms of legal documents and contracts:

    ☐ ____ A. I consider myself quite capable of reading and understanding such documents, and am able to do it quite easily.

    ☐ ____ B. I find reading and understanding such documents difficult and prefer to have someone else do it.

5. To me, being on time for meetings:

    ☐ ____   A. Is critical; I'm uncomfortable if I am not punctual.

    ☐ ____   B. Is not really that important, as long as I get there somewhere close to the beginning.

6. I have an easier time learning:

    ☐ ____   A. The words of a new song.

    ☐ ____   B. The melody of a new song.

7. With respect to dreams:

    ☐ ____   A. I dream very little or generally don't remember them.

    ☐ ____   B. I dream most nights and commonly remember them.

8. In discussing issues:

    ☐ ____   A. I am generally articulate and able to find the right words.

    ☐ ____   B. I commonly have difficulty in finding the right words.

9. In considering my dancing ability:

    ☐ ____   A. I have to be repeatedly shown the correct steps and practice frequently.

    ☐ ____   B. I just have to watch for a few minutes before joining in; it comes naturally, I don't have to practice much.

10. In my professional life:

    ☐ ____   A. I would never rely on hunches in making a decision.

    ☐ ____   B. I frequently rely on my intuition in determining my course of action.

11. In thinking back to childhood school mates:

    ☐ ____   A. I can recall names more easily than the faces that go with them.

    ☐ ____   B. I can picture faces more easily than I can remember their names.

12. If asked to rearrange the furniture in a room for maximum efficiently:

    ☐ ____   A. I would carefully measure the room and the pieces of furniture, then sit down and make a scale drawing.

    ☐ ____   B. I would look over the situation and begin moving pieces into place.

13. In describing my bedroom:

    ☐ ____   A   I would say that it is generally very neat and tidy.

    ☐ ____   B. Generally, it is not something to show the guests!

14. If I relax, close my eyes, clasp my hands in my lap, and then look at my thumbs:

    ☐ ____   A. My right thumb is on top of my left.

    ☐ ____   B. My left thumb is on top of my right.

    ☐ ____   C. My thumbs are tip to tip.

15. With respect to predicting future events and having them come true:

    ☐ ____   A. I have never predicted the future without supporting data and facts.

    ☐ ____   B. I have predicted future events, even though at the time I had no data to support my projections.

16. Given the task of sketching from memory an accurate map of the four states nearest to the one I live in:

    ☐ ____   A. I would have a difficult time of it.

    ☐ ____   B. I could do a reasonably good job.

17. When putting together kits, such as toys, household items, etc.:

    ☐ ____   A. I carefully read the instructions and follow them step by step.

    ☐ ____   B. I look at the pictures or just start putting them together.

18. In buying a major item, such as a car, my approach is:

    ☐ ____   A. I carefully go through magazines and reports to compare technical data and statistics.

    ☐ ____   B. I simply go out, try out a few models, and buy the one I feel most comfortable with.

19. In going away on a short trip, I like my preparation and ultimate departure to be:

    ☐ ____   A. Well planned and organized with "everything in its place."

    ☐ ____   B Nothing special in the way of planning, it "just happens."

20. In watching movies I would say that I am:

    ☐ ____   A. Most excited by action drama.

    ☐ ____   B. Most affected by sad movies.

PART II

Having checked either A or B for each of the 20 questions, you are now asked to go back through each question, and rank each part on a scale of 0 -10. In this ranking, 10 would mean the answer is just like you, and 0 would mean that the answer is totally unlike you. *It is necessary that the two rankings given for A and B must total 10.*

For example, in question 18 if your approach would be to both research the data and try out a few models, then your rankings would be 5 and 5; however, if you would primarily rely on the data, your answer might be 7 and 3, etc.

In completing Part II, place your numerical rankings on the line just to the right of the boxes for each answer.

Note: Question 14 will only have a 10 or 0 ranking.

SCORING INSTRUCTIONS

1. In scoring your Thinking Style Preference Profile, first add the number of As and Bs checked in the boxes in Part I. Since there are 20 questions, your total As and Bs must equal 20. For example, a Part I score might be: 12A/8B.

2. Next, go back through and add together the individual rankings for the As and Bs. Since there are 20 questions with a combined A and B ranking of 10 for each question, the possible combined total of A and B rankings for the 20 questions is 200. (If you checked C on 14, the total possible is 190). For example, a Part II score might be 115(A)/85(B).

3. In scoring the profile, you now have two parts. Using the two examples above, the combined two-part scoring would be presented as 12A:115(A)/8B:85(B).

In presenting the combined scoring it is necessary to always specify (A) or (B) in the second part of the scoring because it is possible that the individual rankings may be reversed from the first part of the score. For example the second part of the sample score given above might have been 85A/115B, in which case the combined scoring would be 12A:85(A)/8B:115(B).

INTERPRETING THE SCORES

The Thinking Style Preference Profile is designed so that the A answers correspond to characteristics commonly associated with a Type A thinking style (see figure A.1), and the B answers correspond to the characteristics of a Type B thinking style.

The *Part I score suggests the overall thinking style preference.* Thus, in the Part I score example given above—12A/8B—the suggested interpretation is that this individual has a *slight* Type A thinking style preference. A score of 18A/2B would be interpreted as having a *strong* Type A thinking style preference. A score of 10A/10B would indicate that the person had no particular preference in thinking style.

The *Part II score is used to indicate the degree of flexibility* or ease with which a person can switch from one style of thinking to the other. As long as the Part

II A and B rankings are fairly equal (less than 125) the suggestion is that the person is very flexible in his/her thinking style. If the Part II score exceeds 125, then the suggestion is that the person is somewhat "locked" into the style of thinking having the higher score, and tends to use that mode of thinking for approaching all kinds of tasks, *even when working on tasks which might be more appropriately solved using the opposite thinking style*. The higher the number, the stronger the indication is that the person tends to use one thinking style to the exclusion of the other. A rough scale would be:

100-125	flexible thinking style, uses both types with equal ease
125-150	somewhat inflexible in thinking style, tends to see things somewhat from one perspective
150 up	very rigid in thinking style, rarely uses the opposite approach

The Part I and Part II scores are closely related. Part I scores that are close to 10 will tend to have Part II scores in the 100-125 range; whereas Part I scores in the extreme, such as 1 and 2 or 19 and 20, will tend to have higher Part II scores.

Most people will want to know what kind of score is "best" or "desirable," but there really *isn't* a best or desirable. You are what you think, and all this profile suggests is the thinking style that you tend to use the most. As long as your thinking style is compatible with the work that you do, it makes little difference whether you have a balanced score or a strong preference in one thinking style over another. On the other hand, if you are having trouble with certain tasks and training or education doesn't seem to be of much help, then perhaps you might want to take a closer look at the match between your preferred thinking style and the required thinking style necessary for the job at hand.

Can a person learn to be more flexible in thinking style? Of course! All it takes is the desire and a little persistence. Becoming aware of a need for change is the most important step.

Should a person become more flexible in his or her thinking style? That's another issue, and a very personal one. Each of us is born with many kinds of thinking tools; how we choose to develop and use them is strictly a matter of choice. The important thing to remember, however, is that good decision making requires consensus between the two hemispheres—if you're a successful 18B:135(B) artist, you might want to hire a good accountant to handle your finances!

Exercise 2

MATCHING THINKING STYLE PREFERENCES TO JOB FUNCTION REQUIREMENTS

Specific job functions can often require particular thinking styles. In this exercise you will analyze each job function within your shop in terms of which thinking styles and approaches are most appropriate for the specific tasks and functions performed on a day-to-day basis. In completing the dominant thinking style column, use the traits listed in figure A.1 for Type A and Type B thinking styles.

1. On a sheet of paper use the format provided in the example below to list the various job positions, functions, and tasks which are required in your shop. Then, after listing the dominant, required thinking style traits which characterize each task, give an overall required hemisphere ranking for each position using a scale of 0 to 10, where 0 is totally type A and 10 is totally type B (5 is balanced). Finally, estimate the average percentage of time that you spend in performing this task. (Note: tasks for a single position or job must total 100%.)

2. Next, calculate the average ranking for your position (in the last column) by multiplying the ranking for each function by the percentage of time spent on that function. Total the results from this multiplication to get the overall required ranking for the job.

3. How does this overall ranking compare with the thinking style preference profile ranking of the person presently doing the job? (Note: to compare the two scores, you will have to divide the person's thinking style preference profile by 2.) How well do these two rankings match? What are the implications of this comparison?

DETERMINING THE OVERALL JOB FUNCTION REQUIRED THINKING STYLE RANKING

Position	Function	Dominant Required Thinking Style Trait	Thinking Style Ranking	X	% of Time	=	Overall Ranking
Customer Service Rep	1) cash register	mathematical, literal, digital	1	x	10%	=	.10
	2) helping customers	verbal, visual, intuitive	8	x	35%	=	2.80
	3) writing invoices	mathematical, sequential	1	x	20%	=	.20
	4) estimating, pricing	analytical, mathematical sequential, concrete, digital somewhat subjective	3	x	35%	=	1.05
					100%		4.15

STRATEGIC FUTURING:
A TECHNIQUE FOR PREDICTING HIGHLY PROBABLE FUTURE OUTCOMES

In a business world of accelerating change, the capability for developing successful, long-range forecasts takes on increasing strategic importance. Flexibility and adaptability to change will ensure survival in the 1990s; accuracy in long-range forecasting will set the standard for success. Strategic Futuring is a simple and highly effective method of allowing you and your staff to explore any kind of business trend or question and predict related events and most probable outcomes. Strategic Futuring can be done by one person but is most effective when used by a group of people, such as your newly-formed self-managing team. When used with your team, not only will Strategic Futuring yield predictions having a breadth and quality of insight that would be difficult for any single person to achieve, but the process itself will serve to strengthen and improve your self-managing team in many ways.

The first step in Strategic Futuring is to formulate the proper question. Since the whole process will depend on the phrasing of the question, it is important that this step be given careful consideration. You may choose to develop the question by yourself or come up with a general topic and then allow your team to develop the proper question as a group.

Once you have agreed upon the central question, write it in the center of your flip chart and draw a circle or box around it (see figure B.1). The next step is to brainstorm for highly probable and significant outcomes which would result from the central question. In the brainstorming phase make no attempt to judge the ideas that the group is suggesting; that will come later. The objective of the brainstorming is simply to generate as many likely outcomes as possible. As each idea is suggested, write it on the flip chart, then circle it, clustering the ideas around the central question. These are level 1 outcomes.

When no more level 1 outcomes are forthcoming, the group should systematically review and evaluate each of the outcomes listed. If *even one*

Figure B.1 ■ **LEVEL 1 POSSIBLE OUTCOMES**

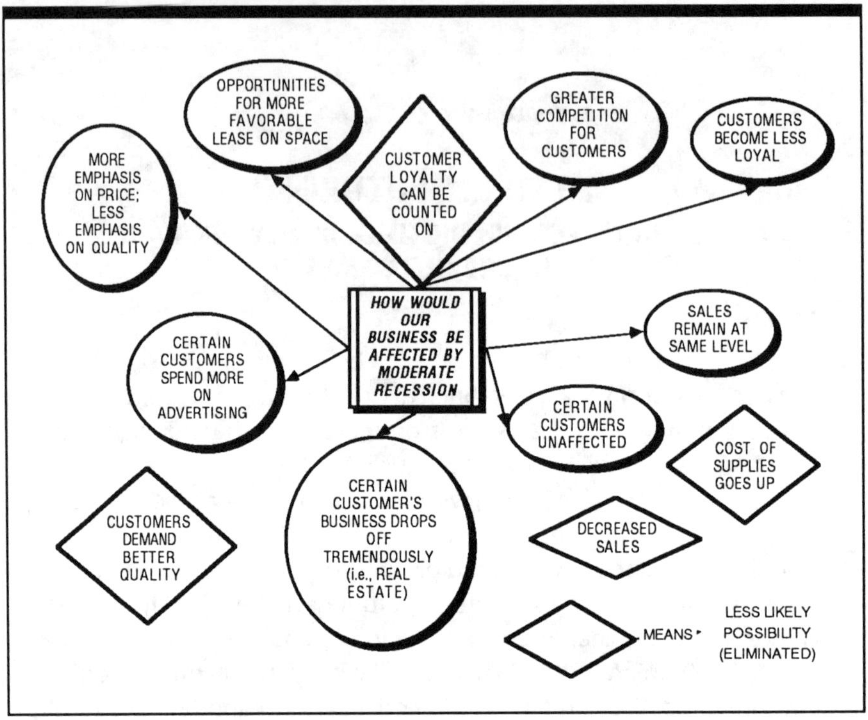

Figure B.2 ■ **LEVEL 1 MOST PROBABLE OUTCOMES**

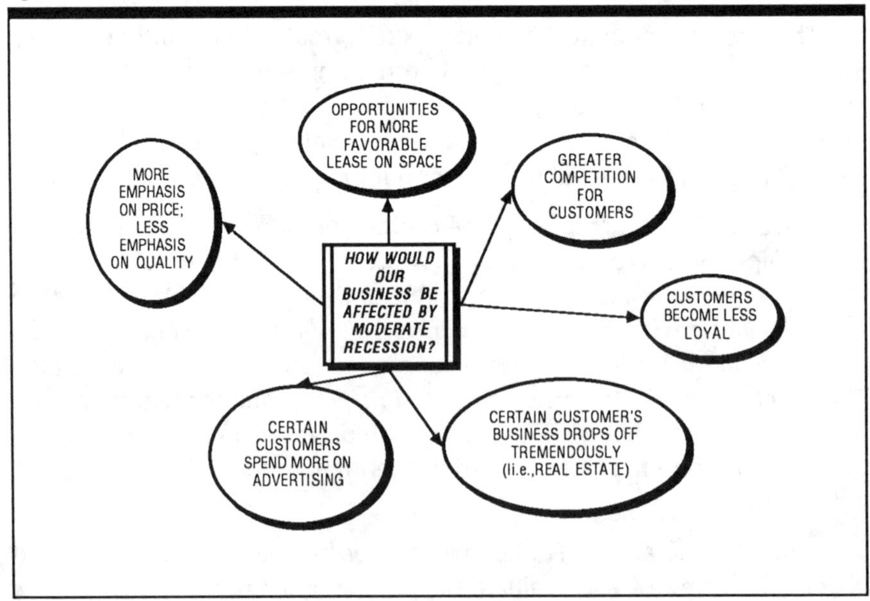

person in the group does not agree that an outcome is likely to occur, then it is eliminated from further consideration. (In figure B.1 four of the suggested outcomes were eliminated.) Once this discriminatory phase is complete, redraw your futuring diagram on a new sheet of paper, with arrows going from the central question to the level 1 outcomes (as shown in figure B.2). This diagram now shows your most probable outcomes. To keep the process manageable, the number of probable outcomes should be limited to between three and six.

Next, repeat the above process for *each* of the level 1 outcomes, generating level 2 outcomes, and then eliminate the less probable ones. Repeat again, generating a third level of outcomes. (Figure B.3 shows the results of Strategic Futuring carried out to level 3 for the original question.) This technique can be carried to as many levels as necessary to fully explore the central question. In practice, however, three or four levels is generally sufficient.

The final phase of Strategic Futuring is interpretation of the outcomes. It is important to note that the resulting synthesis of the most probable interpretation for the original question *already has the total consensus of everyone in the group*, since each outcome had to receive unanimous endorsement to survive. It is necessary to mention this since many times the final synthesis of the futuring process, particularly that stemming from the third and fourth levels, will result in outcomes which are unexpected, unusual, and frequently uncomfortable, allowing the opportunity for denial to raise its ugly head. Figure B.3 started out with a central question that was designed primarily to build awareness within the *staff* concerning the effects of a recession. While this question did not lead to really unusual or unexpected results for the owner, it did result in significant learning for the team, plus a strong buy-in for the strategic action which would be implemented should a recession occur.

The easiest way to illustrate the use of Strategic Futuring is to go through an example. In the example we will use the question Best Image Printing raised in Session 8, *How would our business be effected by a moderate recession?* The following discussion is based on the exploration of this question, as shown in figures B.1, B.2, and B.3.

> *If our business was to experience a moderate recession, three*
> *highly probable and significant results would take place:*
>
> a. *many of our customers would become much more*
>   *cost conscious, and less concerned with quality*
>
> b. *print shops within our area would become much*
>   *more competitive, and*

Figure B.3 ■ **LEVELS 2 & 3 MOST PROBABLE OUTCOMES**

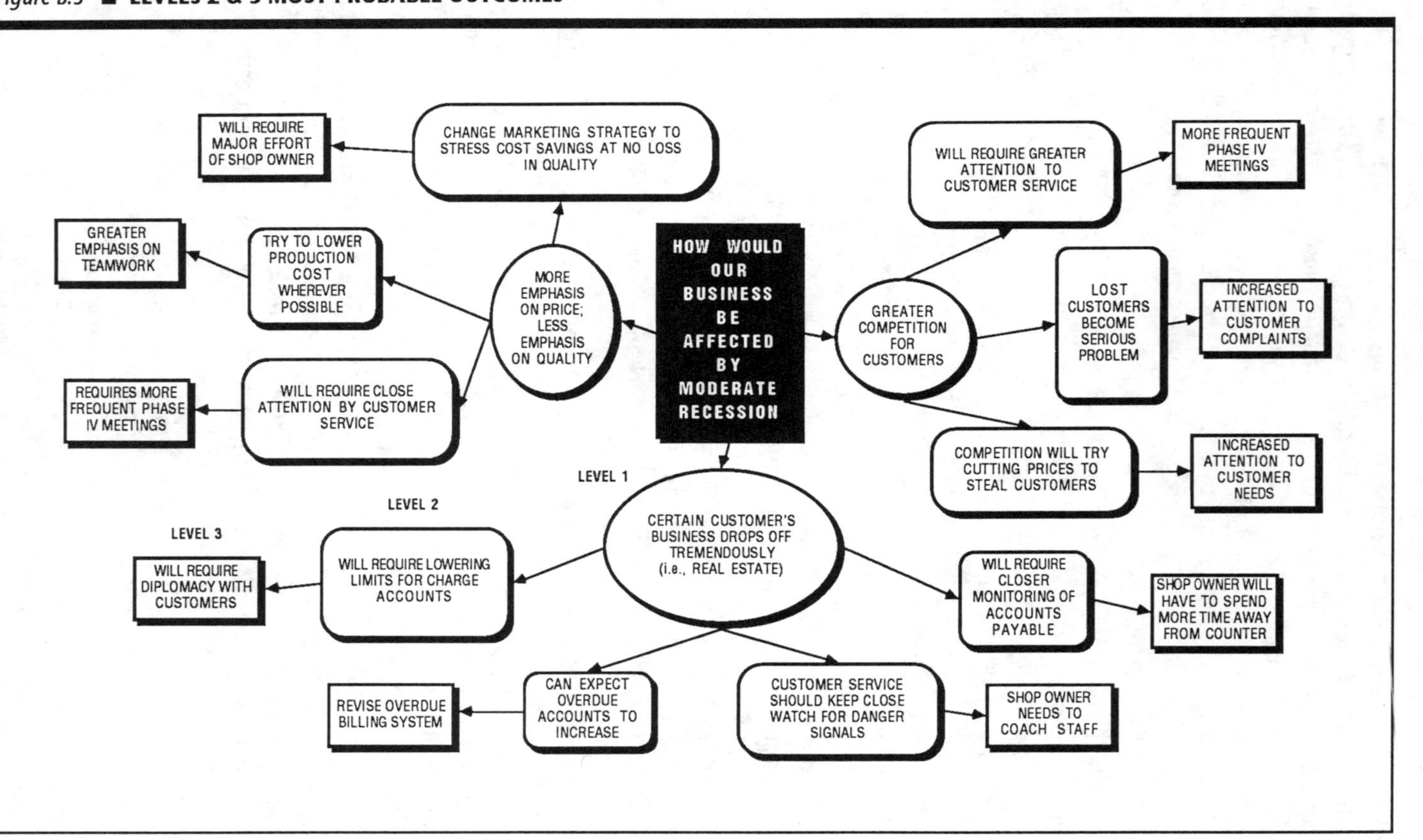

    c.   *certain of our good customers would suffer sharp drops in their business, which would adversely effect us.*

With respect to our customers becoming more cost conscious, this will necessitate certain responses in Best Image, such as: focusing on ways of cutting cost wherever possible, customer service reps giving special attention to customers in pointing out cost reduction options, and the owner critically evaluating our marketing strategy to show our customers that we are trying to help them cut costs. What all of this means is that:

    a.   *we are really going to have to work together even more closely as a team,*

    b.   *we will probably have to increase the frequency of our Phase IV meetings, and*

    c.   *the owner will have to spend extra time away from normal shop duties to work on new marketing ideas, thereby putting more responsibility on the team.*

In terms of the increased competition for customers, we can expect other shops will try to steal away our customers, so we will have to give increased attention to every customer, and every customer we lose becomes a serious threat to each staff member's job! As a result of these outcomes, it is obvious that we are going to have to give great attention to all customer complaints, regardless of how trivial, and increase the frequency of our Phase IV meetings so that we can keep small problems from becoming big ones.

Finally, in terms of a recession's effect on some of our customers, we can expect certain customers are really going to be hard hit, so customer service reps will need to keep their antennae out for signs of trouble. Also, we can expect this to result in an increase in overdue accounts and are going to need to be very careful about extending credit, especially in larger amounts. What all of this means, again, is that we are going to have to be very diplomatic in dealing with old customers if we see a need to reduce their credit, that we will need to implement a closer tracking and monitoring system on all accounts, and that the owner will need to spend considerable time with certain staff members in coaching them in how to deal with these credit and overdue accounts issues.

PATH TO THE IDEAL VISION

The Path to the Ideal Vision is a useful tool for monitoring and graphing improvement in *any* component of a company's overall vision. It can be used for very specific vision components and also for very general and broad vision components. Consider, for example, the general area of quality. You could use the diagram to monitor progress towards achieving an ideal vision of less than 1% press job reworks or to monitor progress towards an ideal vision of being recognized as the best printer in your area.

In explaining the Path to the Ideal Vision diagram to your team, the following definitions will be useful:

IDEAL VISION The ideal vision can represent any component of a company's overall vision. The ideal vision can be the vision of one person (such as the owner) or it can represent a common vision developed and shared by the entire company. In practice, the ideal vision is rarely achieved because it is not a fixed or static vision, but a dynamic concept which constantly evolves and changes as the company progresses towards it.

"NOW" POSITION The "now" position is the existing situation or state of development of the vision component in question. Establishing the "now" position for a vision component can be done in a general qualitative manner or it can involve highly objective and quantitative measurements. The "now" position will serve as the reference point for measuring progress towards the ideal vision.

PATH OF PROGRESS The path of progress is the day-to-day, step-by-step record of improvement and progress towards the ideal vision. The path of progress characteristically plots as a series of ups and downs and plateaus. Rarely, if ever, does the path of progress towards the ideal vision plot as a straight line of continual improvement.

STRATEGIC ACTION PLAN FOR CHANGE The strategic action plan to achieve the ideal vision consists of short-term action plans and long-term strategies developed by the owner, the staff, or a combination of

---

Figure C.1

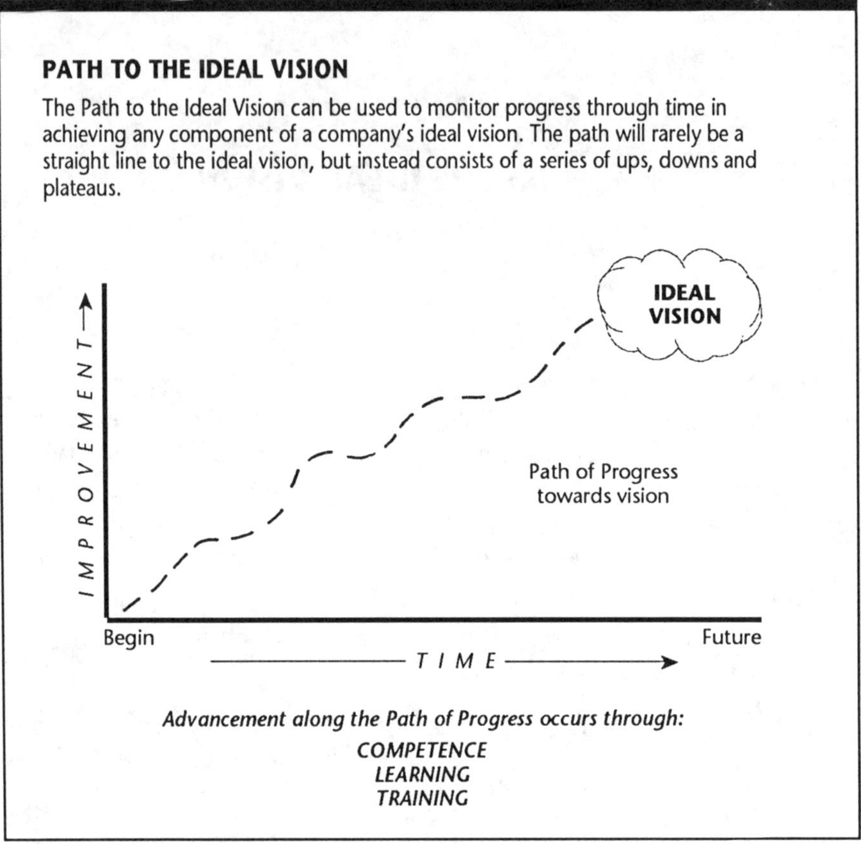

both. A fundamental principal of The MNM Process is that if a company is to be successful in responding to the ever-changing external and internal forces affecting them, then its strategic action plan must be flexible enough to permit periodic reevaluation and, if found to be lacking, revision.

CHANGE IN CRITICAL VISION COMPONENTS In order to move from the "now" position to the ideal vision there must be positive change in critical vision components. Defining precisely *what* these critical vision components are, of course, can be the most difficult part of the whole improvement process. In short, what is required is a definition of *what is the right work*. Often times, when major improvement projects fail it's not because of a lack of effort or commitment, but because the people were focusing on improving the wrong thing. Thus, careful definition of the critical vision components should be given extensive thought and consideration before a strategic plan is developed and implemented.

RANKING SCALE The ranking scale is used to measure improvement in the critical vision components. Different vision components will use different kinds of scales and scale limits. The scale can be highly objective and numerical, as when dealing with vision components which can be quantitatively measured, or it can be quite subjective and verbal, as when dealing with more qualitative vision components. Some examples of various ranking scales would be:

Critical Vision Component to be Measured	Type of Scale	Scale Limits
Number of press reworks	Quantitative (numerical)	0 - 30 % (per week)
Communication between team members	Qualitative (numerical & verbal)	1 - 10 (poorly - well developed)
Develop preventive maintenance system for all equipment	Quantitative (numerical)	1 - 100% (of equipment)
Improve overall vendor relationships (win/win concepts)	Qualitative (numerical)	1 - 100% (of vendors)
Reduce number of customer complaints	Quantitative (numerical)	Number (per month)

PERIODIC MONITORING AND REEVALUATION OF STRATEGY It is essential that periodic monitoring of progress towards the ideal vision take place at regular intervals in order to evaluate the effectiveness of a strategic action plan and make revisions when necessary. It is important that the same ranking scale and procedures be used each time a change in critical vision components is measured. Frequency of monitoring will vary depending upon the vision component being measured. For some quality components, monitoring on a weekly or even daily basis is appropriate, whereas changes in team performance might only be measured every six months.

THE LEARNING CURVE CONTINUUM
A TOOL FOR ANALYZING AND IMPROVING JOB PERFORMANCE

It is ironic how many companies pride themselves in having the latest in state-of-the art equipment, computers, software, etc., yet have no formal system to ensure the on-going training and education of the people that use them. Analysis of this problem suggests that this deficiency often stems from the lack of an effective technique for identifying and quantifying skill and learning deficiencies.

The Learning Curve Continuum is a method for objectively evaluating job function requirements relative to existing individual skill and learning competencies. You can then use this evaluation to develop a long-term strategy of individual skill and learning improvement.

In the Learning Curve Continuum, there are five levels of increasing competency:

Mastery
Proficiency
Competency
Understanding
Awareness

These five levels are diagrammed in figure D.1 and defined below.

Level 1   **AWARENESS**   The first step in developing skill or knowledge in any field is that of awareness. Awareness simply implies that the person is *conscious that a certain technique, process, piece of equipment, or concept exists*. Nothing more, nothing less. It would seem natural that everyone within a company would have awareness of the basic functions, processes and equipment that exist throughout the company; yet it is surprising how often this is not the case. In large companies, a lack of awareness is somewhat understandable (though never justifiable) because of size; but it also exists in companies with fewer than 10 employees.

Figure D.1

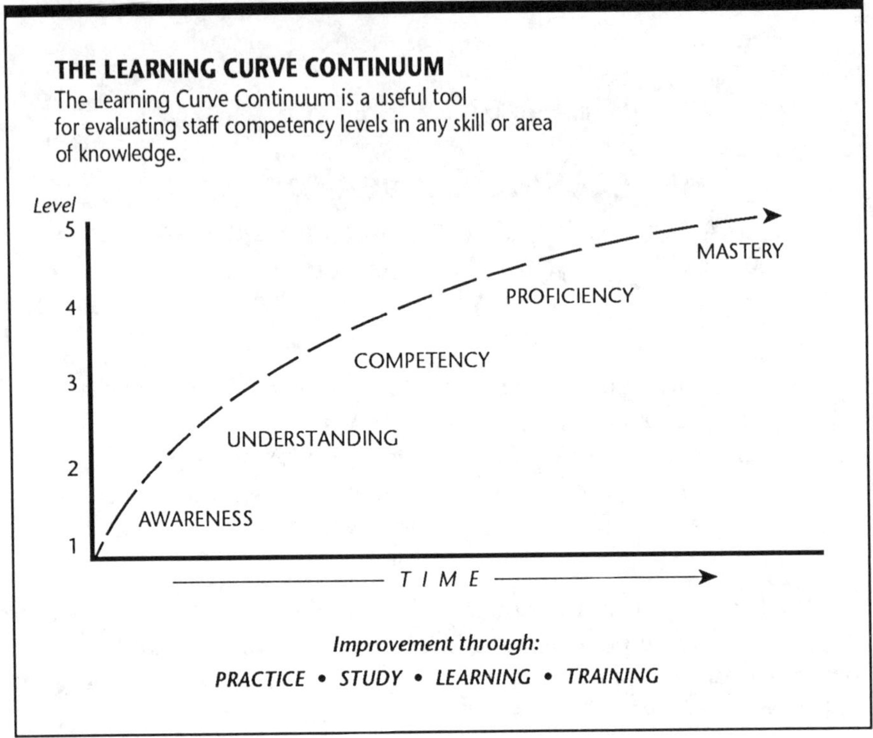

Level 2   **UNDERSTANDING** With understanding comes a sense of the *value* and *usefulness* of a technique, process, piece of equipment, or concept. Also implied is a sense of *why* or *how it works*, along with a sense of its *overall purpose*. The capacity for applying this understanding, however, does not exist. For example, a staff member may have an excellent understanding of the function and purpose of a high-speed copier and its importance to the company's overall products and services, yet have no personal skill or knowledge as to how to operate the machine.

Level 3   **COMPETENCY** The ability of a person to *apply* a technique, process, piece of equipment, or concept in a useful productive manner implies competency. The competency level of skills and learning is the most *basic* level of ability. It is the apprentice or novice level. It also implies the ability to apply the technique, process, piece of equipment, or concept in routine situations. Innovation and creative application are not possible. In the copier example, a person who has developed competency would be able to run the machine to produce routine orders, and possibly do routine maintenance.

Level 4 **PROFICIENCY** Experience, practice and further training and education will, over time, develop a person's proficiency in specific skills or learning. With proficiency comes the ability to *handle or accomplish the unusual and the unexpected.* A person who has developed proficiency should be able to *propose innovative or creative solutions to new problems* on a routine basis. A person who is proficient in high-speed copier usage knows how to maximize productivity, minimize downtime, offer creative options to the customer, and probably handle two or three other tasks at the same time, including being able to jury-rig a weekend repair to finish a critical job!

Level 5 **MASTERY** Not all people will achieve the mastery level of the Learning Curve Continuum, regardless of how much experience, training, or education they may acquire. Mastery implies *special talent* for the technique, process, equipment, or concept. At the mastery level, state-of-the-art knowledge and capability is assumed and action is highly innovative and creative. With mastery a person also becomes an important *resource for teaching* a particular technique or concept. While teaching requires special ability in itself, the replication of the master's talents in others within the company is an important opportunity that should be pursued whenever possible. At the mastery level, our copier operator would probably not have to do the job on the weekend and would anticipate the impending breakdown and have the machine fixed before the failure occurred.

MINDSTORMING

Mindstorming is an excellent tool for stimulating group discussion and synergy, as well as strengthening the overall team. Mindstorming is a special kind of group brainstorming which builds upon the concepts of left/right brain processing to develop understanding and insight that could not be developed by an individual alone into problems, solutions and questions. (See Resource Tool A for an explanation of left/right brain processing.)

In standard brainstorming procedure, the participants are asked to contribute their ideas and thoughts around a central issue or question. A facilitator writes down ideas as they are generated, and usually a surprisingly large number of ideas can be developed within a short time around the central issue. The only guideline is that during the process there can be no judgement expressed by participants (all ideas proposed are listed on the board by the facilitator, even ones that some participants might consider silly or irrelevant). The reason for suspending judgement is to encourage new and innovative input by allowing participants to think openly and freely, and build upon the ideas suggested by the other participants, a process which is thwarted if each idea is immediately censored by the voice of judgement! Once the generation of ideas begins to slow down, the various ideas are discussed individually in a discriminatory, judgemental mode, and ideas which cannot stand up to the combined scrutiny of the group are eliminated.

Recent brain research provides interesting clues as to how brainstorming may actually work. This research has shown that the right brain tends to favor new and innovative ideas and concepts, whereas the left brain prefers the known and the proven. Applying this understanding to the brainstorming process suggests that the success of the brainstorming process, in large part, could be due to effective utilization of left and right brain processing. Specifically, the theory would suggest that the idea generating phase encourages innovative right brain input because critical judgement—a strongly left-brain function—is suspended. Since the suspension of judge-

Figure E.1 ■ From Best Image Printing Session 14

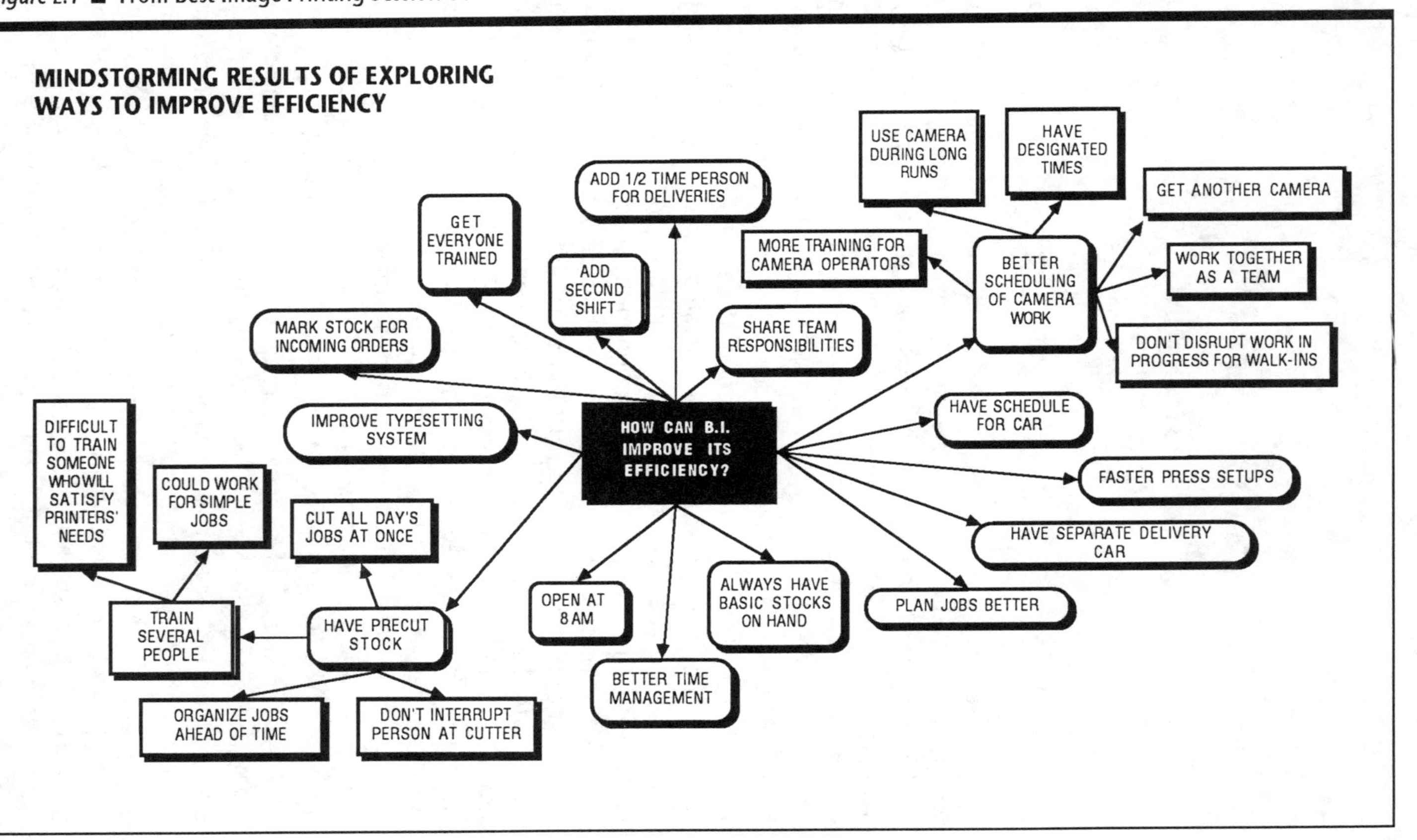

Figure E.1 ■ From Best Image Printing Session 14

MINDSTORMING RESULTS IN OUTLINE FORM

This is the same information that's presented in the mindstorming diagram above. Here it is written in outline form and includes some additional comments that were made but not put on the diagram.

HOW CAN BEST IMAGE IMPROVE ITS EFFICIENCY

1. Add second shift
2. Plan jobs better
3. Open at 8 AM instead of 8:30
4. Have schedule for car
   - pick up and delivery doesn't mean we're a courier service
   - pick up time will influence ultimate delivery date
5. Have separate car for deliveries
6. Make sure basic papers are always on hand
7. Mark stock for incoming orders
8. Faster press setups
9. Share team responsibilities
   - split work where appropriate
10. Improve typesetting system
11. Have precut stock
    a. train several people
       - difficult to train someone who will satisfy printers' needs
       - could work for simpler jobs
    b. cut all day's jobs at one time
    c. organize jobs ahead of time
    d. person cutting stock cannot be interrupted
12. Better time management
13. Get everyone fully trained
14. Add part-time person for deliveries
15. Better scheduling of camera work
    a. More training for camera operators
       - customer service rep A is being trained and customer service rep B will be trained next month
       - when training is in progress, it is essential that other activities be covered by a team member; the person learning the camera cannot be expected to also work at the counter and answer the phones!
    b. have designated times for camera work
       - do camera work at 12 noon every day; work that comes in before noon can be done that day, while work coming in after noon will be done the next day.
       - will require changing lunch schedules
       - have a definite system for covering the counter and doing the camera work
    c. get another camera
    d. use camera during long runs
    e. don't disrupt work in progress for walk-ins
    f. more training for camera operators

ment is *temporary* and the process provides for a subsequent discriminatory phase, the left brain does not "feel threatened," and "allows" these unproven and innovative ideas to come forth.

The above theory, while interesting, is not proven. What is proven, however, is that brainstorming works. It is equally true that when brainstorming is combined with a special type of diagrammatic, map-like visual display which shows linkage between generated ideas, the process becomes even more effective. We can refer to this more effective brainstorming process as Mindstorming.

In Mindstorming, ideas are generated using the same procedure as in brainstorming, but rather than simply listing them in *outline* form, the facilitator places them in circles or boxes which are *clustered around the central idea* (see figure E.1). The linkage lines are added after the judgemental phase has eliminated any ideas which the group decides are not relevant or useful. Generally, a Mindstorming session might include several cycles of brainstorming and judgement in which various ideas and sub-ideas are expanded upon and rearranged.

The advantage of the Mindstorming diagram is that it not only shows all aspects of a problem or question simultaneously, but it links them together in a kind of visual overview to show critical relationships. When the Mindstorming diagram is considered in terms of the right brain/left brain functioning of figure A.1 in Resource Tool A, it is obvious that this kind of *visual spatial mapping and linking of ideas can be considered a more right-brain presentation.* Figure E.2, on the other hand, presents the same information in a traditional outline form which *is distinctly a more left-brain format.*

Depending upon a person's thinking style preference, some participants may have difficulty with the spatial mapping format in the Mindstorming sessions. While the spatial mapping of the Mindstorming approach has the advantage of stimulating the desired Type B input, some very strong Type A people may have difficulty in using or mentally processing the spatial diagram. If this problem comes up, a simple remedy is to prepare the corresponding Type A outline format and tape it up beside the Mindstorming diagram.

Note: For shops that are strongly computer oriented, there is a software program available which is extremely useful for implementing Mindstorming sessions with your team. This program, called "Inspiration," is published by Ceres Software, Inc., Portland, Oregon, and is available from most mail-order software sources. The program runs on all Macintosh computers, allows the user to flip instantly back and forth between the Type B spatial mapping and Type A outline formats, thus accommodating all of the group's preferences. To utilize the program "live" with your group requires an LCD projection plate and overhead projector. The LCD projection plates are not inexpensive, but can be very useful in other applications as a computer teaching aid.

GROUP PROBLEM SOLVING

Group Problem Solving sessions can often provide major breakthroughs and insight on difficult and chronic company problems which could not be achieved through individual pursuit. The reason is due not only to the fact that several heads are better than one, but also because in many, if not most, company problems the human element of the problem is a primary contributing factor. Thus, the simple act of bringing your team together and developing consensus around the general nature of the problem can provide a major step forward in finding a solution. An important spin-off effect from the group problem solving process is that it always results in building a stronger and more committed team.

Considerable research has focused on how the human mind goes about solving problems. Results from this research varies; however, as Willis Harmon summarizes in his book *Higher Creativity*, it is generally acknowledged that there are at least five fundamental and sequential phases involved in problem solving. These phases are conceptualization, input, processing, output and verification, and are explained below.

CONCEPTUALIZATION PHASE The conceptualization phase of problem solving is developing a complete awareness and definition of the problem. In this phase the problem is examined and explored from as many perspectives as possible to carefully define the magnitude, scope, and primary contributing factors. In the conceptualization phase, a critical objective is to *separate the symptoms of the problem from the root causes.*

INPUT PHASE The input phase begins once the problem is defined. The input phase is an *active data gathering* phase where each of the contributing factors, either known or suspected, is *subjected to rigorous objective examination and analysis.*

PROCESSING PHASE The processing phase is a *passive* phase and involves doing nothing for a period of time to give the brain time to digest or process all of the data it received during the input phase. This phase will involve processing by both left and right hemispheres. In short, this phase is basically one of "thinking on it."

OUTPUT PHASE The output phase occurs *spontaneously after an indeterminate period of time* in the processing phase. It is in the output phase that *the brain will suddenly, and often when least expected, offer one or more solutions* to the problem under consideration. Unfortunately, this stage cannot be pushed or "willed" to happen.

VERIFICATION PHASE The verification phase is simply a testing phase where the newly suggested solution is subjected to *rigorous objective testing* and evaluation. Often the verification phase will reveal that a solution is only *partially* correct, in which case the new understanding can be *reintroduced in a feedback loop* to provide greater insight in the conceptualization and input phases.

One of the difficulties in individual problem solving is that the timing of the output phase cannot be controlled. It is true that a person can stimulate the process by "doing one's homework" in the input phase; but sometimes, either because a critical piece of information is missing from individual awareness or because the individual refuses to accept a particular piece of information, the output phase can be seriously delayed.

Group problem solving, however, can greatly accelerate the output phase. With respect to "missing information," more heads *are* better than one, so missing information is more quickly added to the input phase. In the case of "denied information," again, one person may consciously or unconsciously choose to ignore information; this is much less likely to happen in a group of people. As P.T. Barnum noted, "You can fool some of the people some of the some of the time, but you can't fool all of the people all of the time." Thus, the input phase can be more quickly accomplished with a group. But how about the processing phase?

Studies have shown that groups of people working together as a team will more quickly come up with answers that are more *consistently* correct than can individuals working separately. This is especially true if a particular group of people works together frequently. While part of the success of group problem solving is a matter of communication and understanding, another major factor is *being willing to trust*. Certainly, the more a group works together, the greater the degree of communication, understanding, *and trust*.

The exercise that follows presents a group process for problem solving. The exercise is divided into two parts, Problem Definition and Problem Solution. It is designed to bring in the thinking style preferences of all of your team to develop a clear definition of the problem. Once you have clearly and precisely defined the problem, you can begin focusing on the most probable solutions by using the Mindstorming technique (Resource Tool E).

GROUP PROBLEM SOLVING

Part 1 — PROBLEM DEFINITION

Obtaining a clear, precise definition of any problem is always a prerequisite to developing an adequate solution. Indeed, it can be said that the definition of the exact problem is, in effect, the discovery of the solution. Problem definition is best when it involves a synthesis of both Type A and Type B thinking styles. This exercise is designed to utilize the thinking style preferences of all members of the group.

In conducting this exercise with a group of people, the facilitator should write out the problem as it is presently understood. Then, using the format below, the facilitator will lead the group through the following questions in an open dialogue, recording and summarizing the individual contributions on a flip chart.

1. "Basically, the problem which we need to solve is:"

    ____

    "or, to put it another way:" (Here the group should volunteer alternative ways of phrasing the problem, which are recorded on the flip chart.)

    or, ____

    or, ____

    or, ____

2. "In thinking about the problem, let's list your input in these two categories." (Here the facilitator will make two headings on the flip chart and record the input from the group.)

    The way things are now: The way things should be:

    1. _______________________   1. _______________________

    2. _______________________   2. _______________________

    3. _______________________   3. _______________________

    4. _______________________   4. _______________________

3. "Next, close your eyes for three minutes and visualize the most satisfactory outcome to the problem. When you're ready, write down what you experienced. When everyone is done, we'll share and record our answers on the flip chart."

4. "Let's analyze the problem again. Can it be broken down into parts, contributing factors or sub-problems? Take a few minutes to write down your answers and then we will share and record them." (After all the group's individual answers have been listed on the flip chart, the facilitator should go through them with the group to consolidate the answers and eliminate duplications. When this is done, the individual parts should be re-listed and numbered for the next task.)

1. _________________________   5. _________________________

2. _________________________   6. _________________________

3. _________________________   7. _________________________

4. _________________________   8. _________________________

5. "Now, if we take the list of sub-problems or parts and focus on them, our next task is to rank them by their number and a descriptive word or two on the "problem bull's eye." In this arrangement the center of the bull's eye is the *core or most important issue* of the problem and the outer rings are the *peripheral or secondary aspects* of the problem." (Here the group will first do the ranking on an individual basis, and then the individual scores will be combined after discussion to produce a ranking based on the group consensus.)

6. "Finally, taking all of the above into consideration, the last task is for each of you to write, in a single sentence and as specifically and precisely as possible, an exact and true statement of the problem. When you are finished, we will share and record our answers again on the flip chart and then using group consensus, combine them into a single group statement of the problem."

____

____

____

____

____

____

Part 2 — PROBLEM SOLUTION

In most cases, the final statement of the problem which results from the Problem Definition will be considerably more precise than the problem as originally proposed at the beginning of the exercise. Equally important is the fact that this statement will have the support of the entire group. With this consensus of purpose, all members of the team are now empowered to work *together* in finding a solution to the problem.

Once the problem is defined as clearly as possible, the next step is to identify the most probable *causes* for the problem. The Mindstorming technique described in Resource Tool E is a very useful group technique for achieving this objective.

Begin by writing an abbreviated statement of the problem in the center of a flip-chart page. For illustration purposes, let's use the following problem: Why do we continue to lose old customers?

Then ask the group to name all of the major factors contributing to this problem. As the participants call out these major factors (personnel, equipment, materials, quality, etc.), they should be listed around the central problem. Each of these major categories is then considered individually (eliminating those considered unlikely) and a second level of more specific causes is solicited from the group. In this manner successive levels of increasingly specific causes for the problem can be identified, until the group runs out of suggestions.

At this point, the group can consider each of the causes one by one to develop a ranking of the most probable causes. Once this ranking is developed, the group can repeat the Mindstorming process for each of the most probable causes, this time focusing on identifying corrective action that can be taken.

Effective Personnel Management Within a Self-Managing Team

The MNM Process is designed to slowly and without fanfare introduce the concepts of self-managing teams over a period of several months. Experience has shown that this approach is generally preferable to "the big announcement on the new company plan." The fact is, the best change is *invisible*. The more change is visible, the greater the chance it will be resisted. Action—not words—is the key.

Handling Reluctant Team Members

To suggest that a shift to participatory management and self-managing teams will be smooth sailing, with all staff members eagerly embracing each new responsibility given to them, would be misleading. There will be problems—lots of them. And one of the problems that will surface sooner or later will be that of handling a reluctant team member.

Most staff members will readily accept the concept of team participation. You probably used some manner of teamwork on an informal basis before you even began The MNM Process. If this is the case, then the seeds have already been sown, and The MNM Process will simply cultivate the ground and provide the right nutrients. Once this is done, your staff should readily respond, and *champions* for the process will begin to emerge to help carry the work forward.

Your staff is not a crop of corn, however, so you should not expect each person to grow and mature in team concepts at the same rate. Each of your staff has their own personal baggage of previous work experience and education. As coach and leader, one of your most important functions is to be cognizant of these individual strengths and weaknesses and act as a resource to help them get past hurdles as they come to them. At some point, however, it may become clear that one or two staff members are not implementing the concepts even though they are participating in the sessions. The transition from intellectualizing and understanding team concepts to implementing them will, for some people, take a great deal of time. Unfortunately, some people will get stuck in this transition and will need extra help.

You can deal with a reluctant team member by using one-on-one coaching sessions between you and the reluctant team member. It is important that these individual coaching sessions are approached positively and in a non-threatening manner. They should also be specific and objective. Present examples of deficiencies that are unambiguous, and if possible, present constructive, alternative forms of behavior and action that the individual can try. (The concept of satisfying internal customers can provide neutral ground for objective discussion.) Ask questions in a friendly manner to gently probe the source of the resistance, and whenever possible give the reluctant team member the opportunity to suggest the solution.

Try to end a session on an up-beat note and always summarize what steps each of you will be taking in the coming days and weeks to correct the deficiency. Written summaries of the coaching sessions kept by both parties are a matter of choice. If the situation improves, they are not necessary. For some staff members they can be counterproductive in that they imply a lack of trust and impart a sense of fear. On the other hand, for staff members who have the problem of selective hearing (that is, hearing only what they want to hear and rejecting the rest), these notes can be a useful tool in bringing about change. Obviously, if the situation doesn't improve and the staff member cannot make the transition to a willing team member, then, ultimately, termination may be the only option. If you should reach this point, then you will most certainly want to have all those coaching session summaries.

Fortunately, self-managing teams can be very effective in minimizing the number of forced terminations. The reason is peer pressure. Teammates can be effective in bringing around the reluctant team player in ways that are not available to the coach. However, as coach you may have to exercise leadership in helping the team understand the dual responsibilities of being a team member: the team works together to get the job done and is also responsible for the continued success of every team member. In a well functioning, sensitive, and caring team environment, most reluctant team members will come around on their own. Ultimately, if they can't (or won't) change, they will terminate themselves. No person likes to be a square peg in a round hole forever.

Initially then, you may have to face some of these more difficult issues in the transition to a self-managing team. However, once the team is you will not have to repeat the process. Coaching and training new personnel in the advantages of teamwork is both time consuming and costly. Fortunately, there is a much easier way, and that is to *hire* them!

Hiring New Team Members

For many company owners, the hiring of new staff can be a difficult and discouraging task. Doesn't it *have* to be that way? Don't you *always* have to go through four or five people before you get the right one? you might ask. Absolutely not! In fact, it is possible to use the hiring process in such a way that each time it becomes a positive and energizing experience.

What's the secret? Very simple. The key is in knowing *precisely* what kind of person you *really* need, being able to *put that person into words*, and then *place an ad that will speak to that person.*

Deciding what kind of person you need to fill a position can be done by the owner alone or with input from the entire team. There are obvious advantages in involving your team; after all, it's *their* teammate!

If you look in the classified section of the newspaper, you will find that most ads tell very little about what the company is *really* looking for. Ads, of course, are expensive, and in an effort to keep costs to a minimum, anything other than the basic facts is generally edited out. The thinking behind this strategy seems to be "let's get lots of applicants, then we can weed through them to find what we're looking for." The MNM Team Building Process would suggest that this is not only false economy, but does little to attract the desired person in the first place. The truth is that good people *are* hard to find; the ideal person for your team is even harder. To reach that ideal person, the ad needs to *speak directly to that person as an individual.* Help wanted ads should be different from other forms of advertising because you are really speaking to the core of everything that a person stands for; and, if you think about it, the product you are offering is your *combined future.* So looking at it in this sense, the entire hiring process, which includes your help wanted ad, is a critical part of team building.

Below are examples of help wanted ads which were used successfully by Best Image Printing in obtaining their ideal person. When you read them, you'll realize that these aren't average, orthodox help wanted ads. But, then, neither were the people who were hired! The Best Image ads bring in both the special needs of the position, as well as the company team philosophy. For comparison, traditional ads are also included.

Best Image Printing
<u>Help Wanted Ad For Press Operator</u>

Printers: Are you tired of baby-sitting an automatic press all day or night? Are you looking for an opportunity where you can put your creative talents to daily use on demanding work in which you can take pride? If so, we are looking for one additional professional printer who will be satisfied by meeting the challenge of producing high quality work in a team-oriented small commercial printshop which takes pride in delivering the best work in town.

If you're that person, call Best Image Printing.

<u>Traditional Ad for Press Operator</u>

Press Operator for quality oriented small commercial printer. Experienced with Print-rite 2000 presses. Full-time permanent day position with benefits. Call Best Image Printing for an interview.

Best Image Printing
<u>Ad For Customer Service Rep/Copier Person</u>

PRINTSHOP Customer Service/Copier Person: Do you enjoy doing 2 or even 3 things at one time? Can you work close to the speed of light while maintaining a discriminating eye for uncompromising quality and excellence in product and customer service? Can you keep smiling while mentally shifting gears at the drop of a paper clip? If so, we are looking for a special person who will be satisfied by meeting the challenge of producing high quality work in a team-oriented small commercial printshop which takes pride in delivering the best work in town.

If you're that person, call Best Image Printing.

<u>Traditional Ad for CRS/Copier Person</u>

Print Shop Copier Operator: Full-time position involving customer contact and high-speed copier operation. Previous experience desired. Good salary and benefits. Small, well-established shop. Call Best Image Printing for an interview.

Best Image Printing
<u>Ad for Graphic Designer/Typesetter</u>

Are You Creative? Can you type 100+ wpm? Do you have a good sense of aesthetics? Do you have an existing passion for or maybe a secret desire to design printed materials? Do you like working with people in a team environment? Are you presently in a dead-end position? If you can answer "yes" to these questions, we may have lots to talk about! Call Best Image Printing for appointment.

<u>Traditional Ad for Typesetter</u>

Typesetter/Graphic Designer: Minimum 3 years experience in all areas of typesetting and paste-up. Position requires excellent typing skills, self-motivation and customer relations skills. Please send resume to Best Image Printing.

In comparing the examples above, it is obvious that the Best Image Printing MNM Process ads are different. What is it that set them apart and made them successful? For one thing, the Best Image MNM Process ads speak directly to the reader by asking questions in a very personal way. The questions are not patronizing, but actually focus of identifying critical points in common between the potential employee and the overall company philosophy. Another important fact is that none of the ads mention salary or benefits, yet they leave the reader with the understanding that this would be a desirable place to work. The understanding is very implicit that Best Image Printing places great value in its staff and in helping the potential employee achieve *his or her needs,* as opposed to the traditional ads which primarily stress the *company's needs* (i.e., if you meet *our* needs then we're willing to pay you).

BOOKS YOU MIGHT WANT TO READ

PHASE I

Adizes, Ichak, "Getting To Prime." *Inc.* magazine (January 1991): p. 27-33.

Bennis, Warren, *On Becoming A Leader.* Reading, Ma.: Addison Wesley, 1989.

Gerber, Michael E., *The E Myth: Why Most Businesses Don't Work and What To Do About It.* Ballinger Pub. Co., 1986.

Goldratt, Eliyahu M. and Cox, Jeff, *The Goal: A Process of Ongoing Improvement.* Croton-on-Hudson, N.Y.: North River Press, 1986.

Hawkins, Paul, *Growing A Business.* New York: Fireside, 1987.

Kanter, Rosabeth Moss, *The Change Masters.* New York: Simon and Schuster, 1983.

Peters, Thomas, *Thriving on Chaos.* New York: Harper and Row, 1987.

Peters, Thomas and Waterman, Robert Jr., *In Search of Excellence.* New York: Warner Books, 1982.

Sinetar, Marsha, *Do What You Love, The Money Will Follow.* Mahway, N.J.: Paulist Press, 1987.

Stewart, John C., *A Quick Printer's Checklist for Survival in the 1990s.* W. Melbourne, Fl.: QP Consulting, 1990.

Toffler, Alvin, *Powershifts.* New York: Bantam Books, 1990.

PHASE II

Bennis, Warren, *On Becoming A Leader.* Reading, Ma.: Addison Wesley, 1989.

Carse, James P., *Finite and Infinite Games.* New York: Ballentine, 1986.

Deming, W. Edwards, *Out of the Crisis.* MIT Center for Advanced Engineering Study, 1986.

Dumaine, Brian, "Who Needs A Boss." *Fortune* magazine (May 7, 1990): p. 52-60.

Fournies, Ferdinand F., *Why Employees Don't Do What They're Supposed To Do and What To Do About It.* Blue Ridge Summit, Pa.: Tab Books, 1988.

Gerber, Michael E., *The E Myth: Why Most Businesses Don't Work and What To Do About It.* Ballinger Pub. Co., 1986.

Hawkins, Paul, *Growing A Business.* New York: Fireside, 1987.

Kanter, Rosabeth Moss, *The Change Masters*. New York: Simon and Schuster, 1983.

Miller, William C., *The Creative Edge*. Reading, Ma.: Addison Wesley, 1987.

Owens, Thomas, "The Self-Managing Work Team." *Small Business Reports* (February 1991), p. 53-65.

Peters, Thomas and Waterman, Robert Jr., *In Search of Excellence*. New York: Warner Books, 1982.

Scherkenbach, William W., *The Deming Route to Quality and Productivity*. Washington, D.C.: CEEPress Books, 1988.

Stewart, John C., *A Quick Printer's Checklist for Survival in the 1990s*. W. Melbourne, Fl.: QP Consulting, 1990.

PHASE III

Beale, Lucy and Fields, Rick, *The Win/Win Way*. New York: Harcourt Brace Jovanovich, 1987.

Carse, James P., *Finite and Infinite Games*. New York: Ballentine, 1986.

Owens, Thomas, "The Self-Managing Work Team." *Small Business Reports* (February 1991), p. 53-65.

Ray, Michael and Myers, Rochelle, *Creativity in Business*. New York: Doubleday, 1986.

PHASE IV

Goldratt, Eliyahu M. and Cox, Jeff, *The Goal: A Process of Ongoing Improvement*. Croton-on-Hudson, N.Y.: North River Press, 1986.

Peters, Thomas, *Thriving on Chaos*. New York: Harper and Row, 1987.

Peters, Thomas and Waterman, Robert Jr., *In Search of Excellence*. New York: Warner Books, 1982.

PHASE V

Goldratt, Eliyahu M. and Cox, Jeff, *The Goal: A Process of Ongoing Improvement*. Croton-on-Hudson, N.Y.: North River Press, 1986.

Peters, Thomas, *Thriving on Chaos*. New York: Harper and Row, 1987.

RESOURCE TOOL A

Edwards, Betty, *Drawing on the Right Side of the Brain*. Los Angeles: J.P. Tarcher, 1979.

Herrman, Ned, *The Creative Brain*. Reading, Ma.: Addison Wesley, 1987.

Loy, David, *The Sphinx and the Rainbow*. Boulder: Shambhala Publications, 1983.

Russell, Peter, *The Brain Book*. New York: E.P. Dutton, 1979.

Springer, Sally P. and Deutsch, Georg, *Left Brain, Right Brain*, 3rd ed. San Francisco: W.H. Freeman, 1989.

RESOURCE TOOL F

Harman, Willis and Rheingold, Howard, *Higher Creativity: Liberating the Unconscious for Breakthrough Insights*. Los Angeles: Tarcher Publishing, 1984.

RESOURCE TOOL G

Bennis, Warren, *On Becoming A Leader*. Reading, Ma.: Addison Wesley, 1989.

Bibliography

Beale, Lucy and Fields, Rick, *The Win/Win Way.* New York: Harcourt Brace Jovanovich, 1987.

Deming, W. Edwards, *Out of the Crisis.* MIT Center for Advanced Engineering Study, 1986.

Edwards, Betty, *Drawing on the Right Side of the Brain.* Los Angeles: J.P. Tarcher, 1979.

Harman, Willis and Rheingold, Howard, *Higher Creativity: Liberating the Unconscious for Breakthrough Insights.* Los Angeles: Tarcher Publishing, 1984.

Loy, David, *The Sphinx and the Rainbow.* Boulder: Shambhala Publications, 1983.

Peters, Thomas, *Thriving On Chaos.* New York: Harper and Row, 1987.

Peters, Thomas and Waterman, Robert Jr., *In Search of Excellence.* New York: Warner Books, 1982.

Sinetar, Marsha, *Do What You Love, The Money Will Follow.* Mahway, N.J.: Paulist Press, 1987.

Springer, Sally P. and Deutsch, Georg, *Left Brain, Right Brain,* 3rd ed. San Francisco: W.H. Freeman, 1989.

Toffler, Alvin, *Powershifts.* New York: Bantam Books, 1990.

AUTHORS

MICHAEL P. O'CONNOR has enjoyed a diverse career as a business consultant, teacher, and entrepreneur. As a consultant to both large and small businesses, Michael has been developing and implementing the concepts of participative management and self-managing teams for many years. He is a partner in The COS Group International, a Portland, Maine, consulting firm specializing in organizational effectiveness through total quality, strategic planning, and self-managing teams. If you would like to talk with Michael about The MNM Process, please call him at (207) 772-8886. When not working with businesses, Michael can be found playing Irish jigs and reels with his fiddle on his Lord Nelson cutter sailboat, the *Kimberly Laura*.

BECKY ERICKSON became involved in the printing industry in 1975. From 1975 to 1986 she managed the Burlington, Vermont, Sir Speedy Printing Center, which was one of the franchise's Top 25 centers from 1979 to 1984. In 1987 she relocated to Portland, Maine, and opened her own Sir Speedy franchise, which she operates efficiently and profitably, using all of the concepts described in *The MNM Team Building Process for Printers*. If you would like to talk with Becky about The MNM Process, please call her at (207) 761-0041. When she is not working in her Sir Speedy Center, Becky can be found learning to play Irish jigs and reels on her button accordian.

PRODUCTION NOTES

This book and its cover were produced entirely on Macintosh computers. The writing and editing was done in Microsoft Word; those files were then brought into PageMaker 4.0 for page layout. The text of the book is set in Stone Sans, and the output (with the exception of a few of the figures) was done on an Apple Laserwriter II NTX. The cover was designed in Quark Xpress and output directly to color-separated film.

INDEX

A

Adding a new team member 159
Agenda
    for Best Image on-going meetings 150
    for staff meetings 79
    owner's 80

B

Basic responsibilities of team members 121–122
Beale, Lucy & Rick Fields 97
Ben and Jerry 23
Bennis, Warren 5
Berra, Yogi 18
Best Image Printing
    agenda for on-going meetings 150–152
    background 85
    help wanted ads 226
    long-term strategy 69
        revisions to 174–179
    mindstorming diagram 140, 214
    mindstorming outline 141, 215
    minutes from on-going meetings 154–157
    mission statement 20, 34
    strategic futuring 201–203
    strategy 20
        for competition 68
        for customers 62
        for equipment 65
        for marketing & sales 68
        for physical facilities 64
        for products & services 60
        for staff 66
        for vendors 67
    Task 1 agenda 85
    Task 1 sessions
        competition 103–105
        current economic outlook 110–111
        customers 100–101
        equipment 90–91
        marketing & sales 106–107
        physical facilities 87–88
        products & services 93–95
        vendors 97–98
    Task 2 sessions
        creating vision of ideal team 128–129
        individual learning needs 137–139
        individual visions of ideal team 123–125
        mindstorming to improve efficiency 143
        team improvement process 132–134
        using metaphors 117–119
    Ten key characteristics of ideal company
        team 129
        ranking of (9 months after session
            11) 161
        ranking of (session 11) 129, 161
    vision statement 20, 46
        for competition 46
        for equipment 44
        for ideal customer base 43
        for marketing & sales 45
        for physical facilities 43
        for products & services 41
        for staff 44
        for vendors 45
    vision worksheet
        ideal customer base 40
        products & services 38
Brainstorming 81, 199, 213
Building the team 9–10
Burr, Donald 23

C

Cadillac 56
Competition
    creating vision for 45
    strategy for 68
Correlation matrix 168–169
    diagram of 170
    how to read 171
Cycles of on-going improvement 167, 179
    diagram of 178

D

Decision making styles 51, 169
    chart of 52
Deming Prize 56
Deming, W. Edward 56

E

Edwards, Betty 188
Effective personnel management 159, 171,
    186, 223
Equipment
    creating vision for 43
    strategy for 63

PLEASE SEND ME ANOTHER COPY
OF
THE MNM TEAM BUILDING PROCESS FOR PRINTERS!

I have enclosed a check or money order for $42.95 per book.
($39.95 plus $3.00 for postage & handling)
(Maine residents please add $2.00 per book for state sales tax)

Name ____

Company ____

Address ____

City/State/Zip ____

Please mail this form along with your check to:

OLD STONE PUBLISHING
P.O. Box 7572 • Portland, ME 04112

CONSULTING SERVICES

The MNM Team Building Process for Printers, as presented in this book, has been developed as a stand-alone, self-directed process.

Consulting services are available for the business owner who thinks that their company would benefit from additional expertise in facilitating or implementing the concepts presented here.

For further information, please call or write:

MICHAEL P. O'CONNOR
The COS Group International
P.O. Box 7572 • Portland, Maine 04112
(207) 772-8886